JACK-O'-LANTERN

The Strange History of the Halloween Pumpkin From Ancient Times to the Present

Young Boy and Jack-O'-Lantern, c. early 1900s

JACK-O'-LANTERN

The Strange History of the Halloween Pumpkin From Ancient Times to the Present

by
David Acord

Copyright © 2018 by David Acord.

Harris-Jacobson Publishing

All photos and images are © their respective copyright holders. A good-faith effort was made to credit images where possible. If there is an error, contact the author via email at dacord8@gmail.com

All rights reserved. No part of this book may be reproduced, scanned, or distributed in any printed or electronic form without permission.

First Edition: October 2018

Oh, fruit loved of boyhood! the old days recalling,
When wood-grapes were purpling and brown nuts were falling!
When wild, ugly faces we carved in its skin,
Glaring out through the dark with a candle within!
When we laughed round the corn-heap, with hearts all in tune,
Our chair a broad pumpkin,—our lantern the moon,
Telling tales of the fairy who travelled like steam,
In a pumpkin-shell coach, with two rats for her team!

- John Greenleaf Whitter, "The Pumpkin"

Shutterstock/Everett Collection

Table of Contents

Introduction ix

Part One: Before the Pumpkin: Roots of the Jack-O'-Lantern....1

   Chapter One: Spooky Lights at a Distance 3

   Chapter Two: Science Meets Folklore 14

   Chapter Three: The Jack-O'-Lantern's Faerie Aliases 23

   Chapter Four: The Jack-O'-Lantern, Ghosts and Religion 41

Part Two: Creating the Modern Jack-O'-Lantern 67

   Chapter Five: Jack and the Turnip 69

   Chapter Six: The Jack-O'-Lantern's Faerie Aliases 78

   Chapter Seven: The Jack-O'-Lantern in the 20th Century 107

Conclusion: The Jack-O'-Lantern in the 21st Century 136

Endnotes 140

About the Author 151

David Acord

Shutterstock/Everett Collection

Introduction

If I asked you to describe a jack-o'-lantern, you might say something like, "It's a hollowed-out pumpkin with a carved face and a light inside." And you would be right – sort of. At least, that's how we define a jack-o'-lantern today. But two hundred years ago, your answer would have been slightly different. Rather than a carved pumpkin (which, at the time, was a rarity in Europe and Great Britain, where the jack-o'-lantern was most popular), you would have instead substituted a turnip, gourd, beet or even potato.

But three hundred years ago? Four hundred? Five hundred? Now we're getting into mysterious territory. There would be no pumpkins, turnips or any other kind of vegetable – just a strange, disembodied light floating across murky swamps and quiet, moonlit fields. It would be known primarily as a jack-o'-lantern, but it would also go by many other aliases. It would have nothing to do with Halloween, and its appearance would vary depending on the region. Early scientists – including the great Isaac Newton – would struggle to come up with a rational explanation for its existence. Pagans and Christians alike would claim it for their own and create elaborate legends to explain its existence. It would be a sly trickster in one village – the mythological equivalent of Bart Simpson – and an omen of death and misfortune in another. The tortured ghosts of dishonest farmers, the souls of unbaptized babies, the illegitimate children of faerie kings, the Devil himself – all of them have gone by the name of jack-o'-lantern.

Why stop at five hundred years ago? If we search even farther back, we find the ancestors of the modern jack-o'-lantern scattered across history like glowing supernatural jewels. Mysterious lights followed Christopher Columbus' vessel on his second voyage to America in 1493; his crew sang and prayed to them, certain they would protect the boat from violent storms. And yet earlier still, those same lights roamed the seas and hillsides of the Mediterranean alongside ancient Greeks and Romans, haunting sailors and frightening even the bravest of soldiers. In one form or another, it seems the jack-o'-lantern has always been with us, an unreliable companion who is kind one minute and cruel the next, never to be completely trusted.

This book is the first to chart the jack-o'-lantern's long and fascinating history from the mists of legend to its current role as mascot for one of the world's most popular holidays. It has been a long, strange journey to say the least. The jack-o'-lantern has found its greatest recognition in America, which is somewhat fitting because there is a certain restlessness to its story, a never-ending cycle of invention and reinvention that mirrors the country's underlying character. The jack-o'-lantern is like a Broadway actor who goes through a dozen wardrobe changes over the course of a single performance. It's a shape-shifter, constantly altering its form, name and personality. Is it pagan or Christian? Both. Is it American, British or European? Yes, to all three. And what exactly does it look like? Well, as we have just seen, that depends on what century you're talking about.

Most books written on the history of Halloween devote only a few paragraphs to the jack-o'-lantern. There's usually mention of a vague old legend about a man who made a deal with the devil and lost his soul, and somehow this transformed over time into the modern jack-o'-lantern…and that's about it. When I read these books as a child, the pieces never quite fit. Why was it called jack-o'-lantern? Why not Bob or Bill? Why was it a pumpkin? What was the carved face supposed to represent? And how did it come to be associated with Halloween in the first place? What was it all supposed to mean? There had to be more to the story. One day, I thought, I'll find the answers and write the book I always wanted to read. Now, after more than half a decade of research, I have.

As our world grows increasingly reliant on technology, the old customs and superstitions of our ancestors have been largely discarded and forgotten. The jack-o'-lantern is one of the last remaining connections to our ancient, non-digital past. It is, you might say, the last faerie standing. And even if we aren't consciously aware of it, we have a deep, elemental connection to these irrational symbols and the long-dead cultures they represent. By tracing the jack-o'-lantern's convoluted history, we are also tracing our own human journey. My twelfth-great-grandparents could very well have lit their own jack-o'-lanterns in remote English villages to ward off evil spirits or as part of harvest celebrations that date back to the Druids. It is a thin connection, to be sure, but one that deserves to be preserved and remembered. The invisible bonds remain.

David Acord

"Will-o'-the-wisp and Snake," Hermann Hendrich, 1823

Part One

Before the Pumpkin: Roots of the Jack-O'-Lantern

David Acord

Chapter I

Spooky Lights at a Distance

During the last week of December 1839, a wealthy British gentleman by the unlikely name of Jabez Allies spent several nights tromping around the meadows and fields in the West Midlands region of England. It was dark, cold and wet, but despite the miserable conditions, he was having a wonderful time. Mr. Allies was on a quest, and it would take more than a little bad weather to dampen his spirits.

It had all started five years earlier, in 1834, when Allies was investigating some ancient animal tracks preserved in sandstone in Worcestershire and nearby Herefordshire. He was the quintessential antiquarian and had the financial means to indulge his various interests in history, folklore and science. He had written articles and pamphlets about (among other things) ancient Roman ruins in the English countryside near his home, the legend of Robin Hood and even his own pet theory on how planets moved through space. But while interviewing local residents about the animal tracks, he stumbled across stories of another subject that grabbed his attention: strange, unexplained lights that were often seen moving across the countryside late at night. As it turned out, many farmers and townsfolk had encountered them over the years. They called the lights jack-o'-lanterns.

Allies put a hold on his investigation into the tracks and began meticulously recording the villagers' firsthand accounts. What he heard fascinated him. Young and old, rich and poor, the stories were amazingly consistent, even though the sightings spanned many decades. The lights were almost always described as being similar to that of a lantern – specifically a "horn lantern," which had windows made from thin layers of shaved ox or steer horn (bovine horns are surprisingly translucent). Horn lanterns, often called "lanthorns," were crude but effective, and quite common in the English countryside at that time. The light they gave off was soft, warm and diffuse – very particular, and very different from naked candlelight, lightning bugs or other luminescent insects.

Not surprisingly, many of the people Allies interviewed said that when they first saw the light, they thought someone was simply walking through the fields at night with a horn lantern. But they soon realized they were wrong; it moved too quickly and strangely to be a lantern held by human hands. One farmer said that in 1833, the light appeared about thirty yards away from him on top of a small hill. It moved up and down for three minutes, then zoomed to the ground and vanished. On another occasion, around midnight, he saw it rise out of a ditch and pass in front of his wagon, frightening his horses. He "was satisfied it could not be a person with a lantern, because it went so swift, and also because it did not cast any shadow as it passed the trees," Allies noted. He added that "sometimes they appear near to the beholder, and then, in the twinkling of an eye, at a considerable distance…at other times they will stay for some time near one place, and flit up and down and also move about horizontally, as if a person was looking about for something with a lantern."[1]

A man named Samuel Stead, who lived in a cottage called Pain's Castle near the village of Alfrick in Worcestershire, told Allies that one winter's night, he watched a jack-o'-lantern cavort across the field behind his house for almost ten minutes. Initially he, too, thought it was someone carrying a lantern, but its movements were too wild and erratic; the light shot up several yards into the air, then leaped over an eight-foot hedgerow and disappeared.

Jack-O'-Lantern

A married couple related the following story: one autumn night in 1815, they were walking to a nearby farm when a jack-o'-lantern appeared. They watched it move across a moonlit meadow for several minutes, covering at least a hundred yards. It "moved in a gliding way up a down, and made a kind of arch in its progress from place to place...it appeared sometimes to have a quivering motion, as if agitated by a breeze," he wrote. An older man was following close behind the couple, also on his way to the farm. When they arrived, he was nowhere to be found, and they had to wait some time before he showed up covered in dirt. He explained that he had bad eyesight, and had followed "what he thought was a person with a lantern, and which had led him considerably out of the way; but that, at length, having called out, and not receiving any answer, he found he had been deceived."[2] Deception and trickery, as we shall see, is a common theme in jack-o'-lantern stories.

Another eyewitness told Allies that he frequently saw jack-o'-lanterns "after wet weather, in boggy sour places, in the winter season."[3] Many of the other sightings occurred in cold, damp conditions, too. This ruled out the possibility that the lights were simply glowing insects, which were either dead or dormant in wintertime. It also meant that if he wanted to see one, Allies would have to dress warmly.

It took a while, but finally, on New Year's Eve 1839, his persistence paid off. Working off of a tip from the locals, he took a position on the upper floor of Brook House, a magnificent stone mansion overlooking the fields around Powick, a small village in Worcestershire, not far from where he had first collected stories of the lights years earlier. "I noticed it from one of the upper windows intermittingly for about half an hour, between ten and eleven o'clock, at the distance of from one to two hundred yards off me," he wrote. "Sometimes it was only like a flash in the pan on the ground; at other times it rose up several feet and fell to the earth, and became extinguished; and many times it proceeded horizontally from fifty to one hundred yards with an undulating motion, like the flight of the green woodpecker, and about as rapid; and once or twice it proceeded with considerable rapidity in a straight line upon or close to the ground." The light itself "was very clear and strong," he added, "much bluer than that of a candle, and very like that of an electric spark, and some of them looked larger and as bright as the star Sirius."

Allies hung around Brook House for several more nights and recorded a number of additional jack-o'-lantern sightings, including a pair of "two very beautiful ones" on January 2, 1840. They rose together from the ground like twin stars before splitting apart. One fell back to the ground and disappeared, but the other undulated rapidly across the field for fifty yards. Unable to contain themselves, Allies and a group of friends ran across the field after it, but it disappeared.[4]

The jack-o'-lantern has had many identities over the years, but what Allies witnessed was its original, primal form. This is where our story begins – not with a pumpkin or a Halloween celebration, but with a ghostly light roaming across the dark English countryside, tempting even the most educated observer to chase after it.

EARLIEST TRACES

The first recorded instances of the jack-o'-lantern are found in seventeenth-century literature. In Shakespeare's *The Tempest*, written around 1610, Stephano accuses the fairy Ariel of having "played the jack with us." Preeminent Shakespeare critic Samuel Johnson interpreted this as "He has played Jack with a lantern… by which travelers are decoyed into the mire" – and indeed, Ariel had just led Stephano and his companions on a wild goose chase through the jungle.[5] This indicates the lights were already well-known to English audiences – Shakespeare wouldn't have included a reference his paying customers didn't understand.

Another early reference dates to 1663, in Sir Robert Stapylton's comedic play *The Slighted Maid*.[6] The character Jack With the Lantern appears in a black suit decorated with glow-worms, a "coronet of shaded beams" over his head and holding a paper lantern with a candle inside. One character describes him as "the evening's false light, which leads stumbling clowns over moors and marshes into bogs and pits." Another character identifies him as a "foolish fire," which, as we shall see, is one of the strange light's many aliases.[7]

By 1828, the phenomenon was so well-known that it was the subject of a major comedic play, *Jack O' Lantern – or, the Harlequin Sprite of the Dismal Swamp*, performed at London's Royal Amphitheatre.[8] No copy of the play survives, but it's interesting to note the connections made in the title: the jack is described as both a harlequin – a brightly-colored joker – and a sprite, a low-level member of the faerie realm. The link is also made between the light and a "dismal swamp," where it was often seen in real life.

WHAT'S IN A NAME?

The etymology of "jack-o'-lantern" – short for "jack of the lantern" -- is interesting. The "lantern" part is self-explanatory; the lights bore a startling resemblance to the glow of a horn lantern. If you squint hard enough, you may also see the faintest hint of a reference to Diogenes of Sinope, the famous Cynic philosopher of ancient Greece, who, legend has it, once walked through Athens holding a lantern in search of an honest man. Ghosts were also known to wander about at night, searching for one thing or another (or one person or another), sometimes with a lamp in hand to light their way. Given the lights' otherworldly appearance, the use of "lantern" may have also been influenced by the tradition of funeral lanterns, which were sometimes carried by a priest or cleric during the procession from the church to the graveyard.

But why "jack"? As it turns out, there was a good reason. The name John and its diminutive, Jack, once carried slightly negative connotations, though linguists aren't entirely sure why. "Generally speaking," Allies wrote, Jack "means a cunning fellow who can turn his hand to anything, as 'Jack of all Trades,' 'Jack and the Bean Stalk,' 'Jack the Giant Killer,' [and] 'Jack in the Green,' [etc.]. As 'Jack Pudding' means a zany, a merry-Andrew, a buffoon, [etc.] the probability therefore is, that the name 'Jack-o'-Lantern' has been derived from this tribe...'"[9]

The 18th-century classical scholar Thomas Tyrwhitt also noticed the trend. "I know not how it has happened, that in the principal modern languages, John, or its equivalent, is a name of contempt, or at least of slight," he wrote. "The Spaniards [use] *Juan*, as *bobo Juan*, a foolish John; the French *Jean*, with various additions; and in English, when we call a man a *John*, we do not mean it as a title of honour. Chaucer...uses *Jacke fool*, as the Spaniards do *bobo Juan*; and I suppose jack-ass has the same etymology."[10]

It makes sense, then, that the name Jack was used to describe a mysterious light that had a reputation for luring people off the beaten path into bogs and swamps. "Jack," in the parlance of the time, was often a synonym for a sly, untrustworthy trickster. Indeed, "jack-o'-lantern" was a common term of derision in the 18th and 19th centuries. Fly-by-night quacks selling potentially dangerous medical potions were derided as "mere Jack and the lantern sort of practitioners."[11] The name was often used in political contexts, too. "At the Congress of Vienna," one British commentator noted in 1855, "Turkey was not considered necessary to 'the balance of power' – that Jack-o'-lantern...which has so often led statesmen into bogs from which they have never been able to extricate themselves."[12] Another criticized French politicians who "turn their backs on the steady luminary of reason, and follow certain jack o' lanterns that lead them astray."[13] In America in 1844, temperance activists were derided for "following jack-o'-lantern lights that have landed them and their cause in the sloughs of a Siberian bog."[14] And in 1892, a Virginia politician sneered that his opponent "is well known as a political Jack o' Lantern – a man who has been everything by turns and nothing long."[15]

Early depiction of jack-o'-lanterns (note the flames on top of the water), 1862.

David Acord

IDENTITY CRISIS

In some areas of England, the jack-o'-lantern was known as jack-of-the-wad, with "wad" being slang for a torch or burning sheaf of straw. There were feminine versions too: in East Cornwall we find joan-in-the-wad, while in Northumberland jenny-with-the-lantern was often seen. Elsewhere their sisters kitty-with-the-candlestick and peggy-lantern roamed as well.[16] But these variations on the same basic theme were just the beginning. Throughout the 18th and 19th centuries it seems almost every village and region in Britain and Europe had, as a matter of civic pride, invented their own nickname for the strange lights that bedeviled them.

There are dozens of other names for the jack-o'-lantern around the world, a bounty of aliases and false identities (we should expect nothing less from such a world-class trickster). In his 1645 poem *L'Allegro*, poet John Milton refers to a "Friar's Lanthorn," or Friar's Lantern, a combination of the jack-o'-lantern tradition and Friar Rush, a well-known "merry devil" or playful spirit.[17] And in his masterpiece *Paradise Lost,* he describes a "wandering fire" that "Misleads th' amaz'd night-wand'rer from his way / To bogs and mires, and oft through pond or pool." In Shakespeare's *King Lear*, a character mistakes a man carrying a torch for a "walking fire," which prompts another to reply, "This is the foul fiend, Flibbertigibet; he begins at curfew, and walks til the first cock" – in other words, the jack-o'-lantern roams from dawn until dusk.

But these references barely scratch the tip of the iceberg. A brief and far from comprehensive survey of other names for the jack-o'-lantern in Great Britain alone would include fire-drake, corpse candle, Ellylldan, Puck (or Pooka), elf-fire (those who followed the lights were said to be "elf-led" or "Mab-led," the latter a reference to the mythical queen of the faerie realm), elf candle, Sylham lamp (named for a parish in Suffolk where the lights were often seen, the "terror and destruction of travelers"), Gillion-a-burnt-tale, Jinny Buntail, death-fires, spittle of the stars, piskies (pixies), spunky, Hoberdy's lantern or Hobany's lantern (perhaps a corruption of the Danish "hoppe," for horse, and a reference to the up-and-down motions of the lights, similar to the cantering of a horse), Barguest (Yorkshire), spunkie, Miscann Manny, Robin Goodfellow, pinket (Allies traced this to the Dutch "pinken," or "wink," and said it "alludes probably to the twinkling motion of the meteors in question"), brenning-drake, burning candle, Dank Will, Dick-a-Tuesday, Lantern Man and Mad Crisp.

Scandinavians called it lyktgubhe, while in Finland it answered to aarnivalkea; in the Netherlands it was dubbed osschaert, while in Germany it was called tuckebold; in France it was known generally as feux-follets, although in Brittany they named it Sand Yan y Tad, or St. John and the Father, "carrying at its finger-ends five lights, which spin round like a wheel."[18] Another related Brittany legend is that of the porte-brandon, roughly translated as "the holder or carrier of a firebrand." This is a spirit that appears as a child carrying a torch, "which he turns like a burning wheel; and with this it is said that he sets fire to the villages – which are sometimes suddenly in the middle of the night wrapped in flames."[19] And finally, my personal favorite alternate name for the jack-o'-lantern: "mucus sneezed from the nostrils of rheumatic planets."[20]

The 19th-century British archaeologist and anthropologist M.J. Walhouse collected several jack-o'-lantern folk-tales from around the world. The Shanar caste in southern India believed in *pey-neruppu,* or devil-fires, demons that moved over marshy areas in the form of flickering lights. He recalled: "Riding late after dark over a jungly tract near mountains I once saw what the natives with me averred was a *pey-neruppu*; it seemed a pale ball of flame, the size of an orange, moving in a fitful wavering way above the bushes and passing out of sight behind trees; its movements resembled the flight of an insect, but I know none in India that shows any such light; the fireflies there are no larger than fireflies in Italy."

Walhouse continued: "A strange kind of ghostly lights, on an extensive scale, is sometimes to be seen in the Mysore province of the Madras Presidency. The great hill-fortress of Nandi-drug rises some 1,500 feet above the plain; the fort on the top includes many buildings and commands wide prospects. It is thirty miles from the large military cantonment of Bangalore, and much resorted to. From the top the remarkable exhibition known as 'the Nandi-drug lights' is now and then seen. Not having witnessed it myself I will copy an account that appeared in a Madras newspaper. The correspondent writes, that being on a visit to the fort, and looking at night from his window, which commanded a wide view over the country below, he was amazed at seeing the whole expanse for miles one blaze of light, the appearance being as of a vast city lighted by gas – hundreds and thousands of lights extending for miles, dancing and glittering in all directions – a weird yet beautiful sight. On asking what was the meaning of it, he was told 'it was the bodies of all those who were killed in battle at Nandi; they all come up at this time with lights in their hands.'"

The *chir-batti*, or ghost light, is also well known in India and neighboring Pakistan, and has been seen in the region for centuries, moving across marshlands at night.

Japanese folklore is filled with tales of jack-o'-lanterns. The *hitodama* are souls that have left their bodies, and manifest as

Jack-O'-Lantern

bright balls of light that float in the night air. *Onibi* are colorful balls of light that hew closely to the European idea of the jack-o'-lantern, and are said to be spirits that lift themselves up from human and animal corpses. They are thought to be disagreeable in nature. The *kitsunebi* is another Japanese "ghost light" that tricks night travelers into wandering off the road and getting lost.

The jack-o'-lantern also roams throughout South and Central America. In Colombia, *la candileja* is the jack-o'-lantern ghost of an evil grandmother who raised her children to be thieves and killers. As punishment, after she died she was forced to wander the earth as a ghostly flame. In Brazil it is known by many names, including *boitata*, which roughly translated means "serpent of fire." The legend goes that a giant snake would attack animals in the forest and eat only their eyes, which gave it a strange, bright luminescence. Meanwhile, *luz mala*, or evil light, stalks rural and remote areas of Argentina and Uruguay. More of a traditional jack-o'-lantern, it is commonly described as a very shiny ball of light that hovers just a few inches from the ground.

Left, the Japanese hitodama; right, kitsunebi.

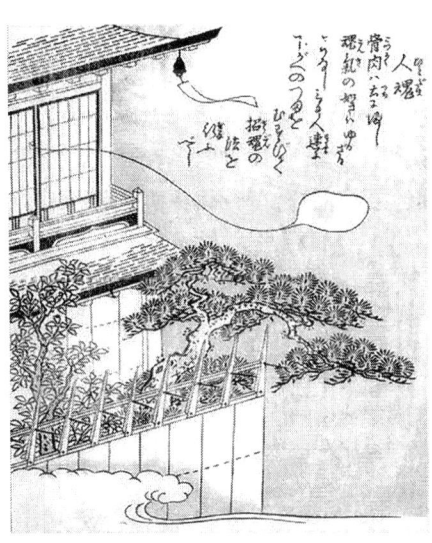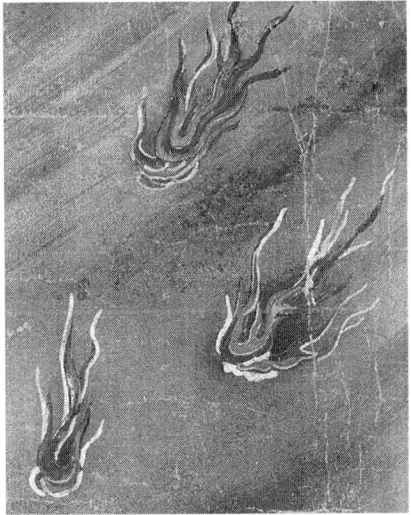

Chapter 2

Science Meets Folklore

Unlike the modern scientific community, which automatically ridicules (or ignores) most "paranormal" subjects like ghosts, Bigfoot and UFOs, earlier generations of scholars took the jack-o'-lantern seriously. In fact, almost as soon as it entered the public consciousness in Great Britain and Europe in the Middle Ages, the educated class – scientists, naturalists and the like – agreed that it was a physical phenomenon and set about trying to find a rational explanation for it. There was little if any debate over whether jack-o'-lanterns actually existed. Until the 19th century, the lights were fairly common and easily observable throughout England and Europe, if you knew when and where to look.

Medieval scholars were the first to investigate the lights. Like any self-respecting community of scientists, they came up with their own sophisticated name for the phenomenon, because using a common term like jack-o'-lantern just wouldn't do. They settled on *ignis fatuus*, Latin for "foolish fire," "wild fire" or "silly fire," a reference to those who frequently chased after the light in hopes of catching it but instead wound up lost and embarrassed. *Ignis fatuus* dates back to at least the sixteenth century and probably quite earlier. Shakespeare used the term in *Henry IV Part I*, written around 1590, to describe someone running through the night like "a ball of wildfire."

Many scientists rolled up their sleeves and went out into the field in search of the *ignis fatuus*. Their written accounts have left us with a priceless database of early jack-o'-lan-

"The Ignus Fatuus or Marsh Light," Mary Evans

tern encounters. In 1728 a scientist from Bologna, Italy, Dr. Giacomo Beccari, penned an extremely detailed description of his investigations, which is worth reprinting in large part:

"I find upon the whole that they are pretty common in all the territory of Bologna. To begin with the plains, they are very frequently observed there… They are most frequent in watery and morassy grounds; and there are some such places, where one may be almost sure of seeing them every night, if it be dark. In the fields near the bridge Della Calcarata…north of Bologna, one of these fiery appearances is very often observed to move across the fields, coming from another bridge, called Della fossa quadra. There is another of them in the fields of Bagnara, almost east of Bologna, which scarce ever fails to appear in dark nights; particularly when it rains or snows; as also in cold and frosty weather. Both these… are very large; and I am assured that sometimes their light is equal to that of one of our ordinary faggots, or bundles made of vine-branches; and that it is scarce ever

"Light of Truth," William Holman Hunt

less than that of the links which our country people make of hemp stalks, and which they light themselves withal, when they travel in the night. [An *ignis fatuus*] at Bagnara appeared, not long since, to a gentleman of my acquaintance, as he was travelling that way; it kept him company for a mile or better, constantly moving before him, and casting a stronger light on the road than the link he had with him.

"I believe there may be several more in other plains, as large as these two," Beccari continued, "though at present I have not been able to get certain information of any others. Lesser ones there appear a good many, some of them giving as much light as a lighted torch; and some are no bigger than the flame of a common candle. Of these I have been assured a good many have been observed in the fields of Barisella. All of them have the same property, in resembling, both in color and light, a flame strong enough to reflect a

Jack-O'-Lantern

luster upon neighboring objects all round. They are continually in motion; but this motion is various and uncertain. Sometimes they disappear of a sudden, and appear again in an instant in some other place. Commonly they keep hovering about six foot from the ground. As they differ in largeness, so do they in figure, spreading sometimes pretty wide, and then again contracting themselves. Sometimes breaking to all appearances into two,  and a very little while after uniting again into one body; sometimes floating like waves, and letting drop some parts, like sparks out of a fire. I have been assured that there is no dark night all the year round in which they do not appear. And in the very middle of winter, when the weather is very cold, and the ground covered with snow, they are observed more frequently than in the hottest summer...Nor doth either rain nor snow in any wise prevent or hinder their appearance; on the contrary, they are more frequently observed, and cast a stronger light in rainy and wet weather."[21]

Despite the sincerity and open-mindedness many scientists displayed toward the jack-o'-lantern, others dismissed the whole phenomenon as a case of mistaken identity and claimed people were just seeing glow worms or other phosphorescent insects and letting their imaginations get the better of them. But this discounted an important fact mentioned by Beccari and many other researchers: a large number of sightings occurred in cold weather, when insects simply weren't around. The claim was also insulting to many of the eyewitnesses who, while perhaps not formally educated, were farmers who had intimate knowledge of the flora and fauna of the countryside. They weren't likely to mistake a common insect for something more mysterious (even if they had had a few too many drinks before the walk home).

RUNNING THE GAMUT

The sheer variety of eyewitness accounts also made it difficult to come up with a neat and tidy explanation. The jack-o'-lanterns showed up in many different colors – blue, green, red, yellow, purple, or combinations thereof – and, as Beccari noted, many sizes too, from tiny pinpricks to large softball-sized emanations. Dr. Thomas Shaw, a popular 18th-century travel writer, recorded one of the more bizarre encounters. While traveling one night through the valleys of Mount Ephraim in modern-day Israel, a shape-shifting *ignis fatuus* followed his party for more than an hour. He wrote: "Sometimes it was globular; sometimes it resembled the flame of a candle; when instantly it would spread itself, and involve the whole company in its pale inoffensive light: then, contracting itself, it would seem to vanish from the sight, but in a few moments would resume its luster, or, moving from place to place, would expand, at intervals, over two or three acres of land. It should be observed, that in the preceding evening the atmosphere had been uncommonly thick and hazy, and the dew remarkably unctuous."[22]

A consistent theme in the folklore was that the jack-o'-lantern lured people into the darkness and remained tantalizingly just out of reach – it pulled away as you moved toward it, as if the light and the observer were mismatched magnets repelling one another. This contributed to the notion that the jack-o'-lantern was a sentient being, a trickster faerie intent on mischief. But this aspect, at least, was easily explained: the motion of the person moving toward the jack-o'-lantern disturbed the air and pushed it – whatever "it" was – farther away. The light apparently had the same miniscule mass and weight

Jack-O'-Lantern

of a spider web or dandelion spore. One 19th-century researcher, a Major Blesson of Berlin, who ventured deep into the marshy forests of Germany to spy on his prey, noted that even "the current of air produced by his breath was sufficient to keep them a little beyond his reach." He solved this problem by standing perfectly still and holding a handkerchief over his mouth. Eventually the lights moved close enough for him to observe them in some detail: blue flames of varying hues that shot up from the bubbling, encrusted surface of the marsh.

Blesson was convinced the lights were some form of burning gas created by the decomposition of vegetable and animal matter in the marsh, the water of which had a high iron content. He conducted several interesting experiments. In one, he managed to hold a piece of paper close to one of the jack-o'-lantern lights. When he examined it later, he discovered that it had been singed and was covered with some sort of "viscous moisture." He repeated the experiment with a smaller strip of paper, and this time it actually ignited into flame upon contact with the jack-o'-lantern!

This finding put Blesson at odds with other scientists – including the one and only Sir Isaac Newton, who called the *ignis fatuus* a "vapour shining without heat." Others had also noted an apparent lack of heat that emanated from jack-o'-lanterns. But Blesson was undeterred. On another occasion, he held a burning torch close to the surface of the marsh in an area where he had previously seen the lights and gas bubbles. "Instantly a kind of explosion was heard over eight or nine square feet of the surface of the marsh; a red light was seen, which diminished to a small blue flame, nearly three feet in height." These experiences convinced Blesson that the jack-o'-lantern – at least the variety present in that particular German forest – was a flammable, combustible gas.[23]

By the early 19th century, a rough, general consensus had emerged that the *ignis fatuus* was caused by some sort of reaction between gasses from decaying vegetable or animal matter and the atmosphere, but that's about as far as it went. One theory pointed to a compound of phosphorus and hydrogen as the likely culprit; as it bubbles to the surface and makes contact with air, a luminescent flame is produced. But critics of this theory argued that "phosphoretted hydrogen," as it was called, could only generate a white flame – not to mention the fact that it also created white smoke rings, which were absent from eyewitness accounts. Methane, or natural gas – a mixture of carbon and hydrogen produced by rotting organic matter -- was another likely culprit. Commonly called "marsh gas" or "swamp gas," it was frequently seen in boggy areas. When decaying matter comes into contact with oxygen, a glowing cloud or flame-like substance is sometimes created.[24] These general theories still hold sway today, although modern scientists hypothesize the lights might also have a geologic origin. Tectonic shifts can cause rock masses to grind against one another, and if these rocks have the right properties, a form of electricity is generated that can manifest on the surface as a ghostly light. These are more commonly called earth lights or ghost lights and have been documented in many areas around the world.

    The most likely explanation is that there were several different sources for the mysterious lights, depending on location, geography, weather and a host of other factors. Some jack-o'-lanterns were likely geologic in nature, while others were caused by several different potent brews of swampy conditions and decaying organic matter. Case closed, right? Not quite! The fact is, none of these theories adequately explain one of the most mysterious – and consistent – aspects of eyewitness accounts. The jack-o'-lantern often moved with seeming animation, if not outright intelligence, over very long distances, veering and curving as if steered by an invisible pilot, often for several minutes or longer at a stretch (recall the story a villager told Allies about the light leaping over an eight-foot hedgerow). Swamp gas and similar phenomena are mostly stationary, hovering over water and wet ground. Geologic shifts might produce electric sparks that move in a more animated manner, but the conditions have to be just right to produce such sparks. It's highly unlikely that vast regions of

THE IGNIS-FATUUS, OR WILL-O'-THE-WISP.

Great Britain and Europe had just the right mix of underground rock to produce so many sightings over the course of several centuries.

LOST FOREVER?

Unfortunately, the mystery will probably never be definitively answered. Most (if not all) of the jack-o'-lantern's prime habitat – fens, marshes, bogs and low-lying farmland – was long ago drained, plowed over and reshaped into suburbs, freeways or large-scale farming operations. The pre-industrial environment in which the jack-o'-lantern thrived, with its unique and fragile set of characteristics, can never be replicated.

By the early 19th century, sightings of the jack-o'-lantern in

Great Britain were rare. A writer in 1828 described it as "this far-famed English apparition, the subject of many stories and the terror of our forefathers, but whose pranks, in consequence of the general drainage of the country, have been of late extremely uncommon."[25]

A news article from 1845 noted, "The extensive bogs and marshes which once covered a large portion of the counties of Northampton, Huntingdon, Cambridge, Lincoln, Norfolk and Suffolk, have now been converted by drainage into fruitful and highly productive land, and throughout the country the same energy which dictated this immense undertaking has been and is at work to redeem waste lands from their state of unproductiveness, and to convert the bog and the morass into solid crop-bearing land. Thus [the jack-o'-lantern] is driven from its old haunts, and the malignant spirit effectually 'laid' by the steady progress of improvement and the diligent cultivation of the soil."[26]

As one Welshman eloquently put it, the jack-o'-lantern "is now starved to death, and his breath is taken from him; his light is quenched forever by the improving farmer, who has drained the bog; and, instead of the rank decaying vegetation of the autumn, where bitterns and snipes delighted to secrete themselves, crops of corn and potatoes are grown."[27]

Chapter 3

Jack-O'-Lantern and His Faerie Aliases

How did our forebears perceive the pre-pumpkin, pre-Halloween jack-o'-lantern? What did they believe its nature or essence to be, exactly? Again, there is no single answer. It was often seen in contradictory terms, simultaneously sacred and profane, as its various aliases suggest. Nevertheless, the list can be broken down into two general categories.

The first is pagan folklore, derived from the ancient faerie mythology most prominent in Great Britain, especially Ireland, Scotland and Wales. In these cases, the jack-o'-lantern was seen as a low-level member of the faerie pantheon – inherently mischievous but not possessing a great deal of harmful supernatural power. These various guises fall into the same class as imps, goblins, pixies, sprites, bogies, boggarts and brownies – minor domestic spirits who specialized in bedeviling farmers and housewives with pranks and acts of petty chaos (spoiling the milk, stealing grain, etc.).

WILL-O'-THE-WISP

After jack-o'-lantern, the most popular name for the lights was will-o'-the-wisp, or "William of the wisp" – "wisp" being another slang term for a burning sheaf of straw or hay. "Will" has a less negative connotation than "Jack," and was probably used as a generic name

The Ignis Fatuus.

for a man (there was a constant effort to personify the lights by giving them human names). However, Allies theorized that "Will" might have been taken from the Saxon *wile*, meaning fraudulent, deceitful, or a trick.[28] It was sometimes further corrupted to Billy-of-the-wisp.

Depending on who you talked to, the will-o'-the-wisp was either a devil or an angel. A woman from the Scottish West Highlands told one Victorian-era writer, "Will-o'-the-wisp is a

Jack-O'-Lantern

very bad thing. It just appears for the purpose of leading people astray and bringing them to their end. There was a man who was out at night, and he saw a Will-o'-the-wisp going before him. He thought it was a light from a house, and he made for it. When he would reach where he thought it had been, he would find it as far away before him as ever. It cheated him in that way for a long time, and the next day he was found dead in a peat bank."

But another woman countered with her own description: "Willie Wisp is plenty true. He's a man that goes running inside fire, here and there, wherever there is to be trouble, and tells people beforehand that it is coming. He does not bring the trouble, but he comes before it."[29]

The Victorian writer T.L. Phipson was an aficionado of the will-o'-the-wisp – in today's vernacular he might be termed a "super fan," the equivalent of an obsessed train spotter or birder. He meticulously catalogued the best places in England to view the mysterious lights and seemed to have spent quite a bit of time crisscrossing the country in search of them. He provides one of the clearest and most eloquent definitions: "Will-o'-the-wisp shows itself on dark autumnal nights as a flickering wandering flame, hovering in the air at a little distance – two or three feet at most – from the ground, or above the surface of stagnant water. It appears sometimes about the size of a man's hand, at others not larger than the flame of a common candle; it will dance wildly about for a few instants, and then become extinguished; at this moment another light of the same kind will show itself, near the same place; and so on for a length of time. Often several 'giddy flames' will be seen at once. If the observer endeavors to approach them, the lights recede; if he rushes wildly away from them, they have sometimes been observed to follow him. Hence these remarkable appearances have oftentimes intimidated the peasantry, and have been attributed generally to evil spirits (elves, according to demonologists, are merely little devils), for it has been more than once recorded that, in endeavoring to follow the Will-o'-the-wisp over boggy lands, some per-

In the late 19th and early 20th centuries, the will-o'-the-wisp was often portrayed by artists in a romantic, feminine form. Case in point: "Will-o'-the-Wisp" by E. Spangenberg, 1914. Here "she" lures a man through the marsh to his eventual downfall.

Jack-O'-Lantern

In children's literature, by contrast, the will-o'-the-wisp was portrayed as a mischevious yet still friendly sprite, usually a perpetually young child.

sons have been engulfed in the morass, and have lost their lives."[30]

Phipson also recounted the following story: "In September 1858 a lady with her little girl and a clergyman were benighted and lost their way on one of the Taff Vale mountains, South Wales. Being on horseback, among dangerous bogs, in intense darkness, they moved cautiously along in search of a road; till, passing a little dell or ravine with a wall at the bottom of it, they saw just across it many bright lights apparently swung about near the ground. They all exclaimed at once 'They have sent out men to look for us with lanterns!' and so firm was this belief that, not being able to cross the wall, the reverend gentleman put his hand to his mouth and shouted long and loud. As the wall was not more than thirty yards distant, the young lady, who was mounted on a Welsh pony, scrambled down to it; when she instantly exclaimed, 'They are Will-o'-the-wisps, mamma, and it's an awful bog!' which proved to be the case for there were no human beings within miles of them. This occurred at eleven o'clock at night and at a thousand feet above the sea-level."

PUCK (POOKA)

Puck, sometimes poake or pooka, is the consummate supernatural trickster and the poster boy for faerie mischief. Thanks to William Shakespeare, who gave the male imp a memorable supporting role in *A Midsummer Night's Dream*, he is also one of the most well-known of the jack-o'-lantern's aliases and was well-distributed across Great Britain. Allies and other 19th-century researchers collected dozens of place-names that referenced the creature: Puck Hill, Puck Lane, Puck Meadow, Puck Croft, etc. Wheat and corn farmers even named a troublesome weed after him: "puck's needle" was a nickname given to the common *Scandix pecten-veneris,* which often infested their crops.

Puck's name is derived from pouk, poker, pocker and a cluster of other Scandinavian-based names for a devil or demon (as well as "the" devil, Satan) that date back to at least medieval times.[31] It is also very similar to the old Dutch "spook." Despite this rather sinister lineage, Puck wasn't seen as a truly evil or dangerous being, though he was still capable of creating a considerable amount of chaos. Puck was a shapeshifter and showed up in any number of guises, not just the jack-o'-lantern. In *A Midsummer Night's Dream* (Act III, Scene I) he describes himself this way (and note the reference to "fire"):

Welsh Pooka

"Through bog, through bush, through brake, through brier:
Sometime a horse I'll be, sometime a hound,
A hog, a headless bear, sometime a fire;
And neigh, and bark, and grunt, and roar, and burn
Like horse, hound, hog, bear, fire, at every turn."

The Puck of Irish faerie lore was darker and more malevolent, part of a "malignant class of beings... preeminent in malice and mischief," according to one 19th-century folklore analysis. "In form he is a very Proteus – generally a horse, but often an eagle. He sometimes assumes the figure of a bull, or becomes an *ignis fatuus*. Amongst the great diversity of forms at times assumed by him, he exhibits a mixture or compound of the calf and goat...he lures but to betray...he deludes the night wanderer into a bog, and leads him to his destruction in a quagmire or pit."[32] Those unfortunate souls who followed his false trails were said to have been "puck-led."

When disguised as a horse, the Irish Puck's overriding goal was to trick an unsuspecting human into jumping on its back. "The great object of the Pooka seems to be to obtain a rider, and then he is in all his most malignant glory. Headlong he dashes through briar and brake, through flood and fell, over mountain, valley, moor, or river, indiscriminately; up or down precipice is alike to him, provided he gratifies the malevolence that seems to inspire him. He bounds and flies over and beyond them, gratified by the distress, and utterly reckless and ruthless of the cries, and danger, and suffering, of the luckless wight who bestrides him."[33] Another Irish variant, the phooka, takes the form of either a black horse, eagle or bat, "and compels the man of whom it has got possession, and who is incapable of making any resistance, to go through various adventures in a short time. It hurries with him over precipices, carries him up into the moon, and down to the bottom of the sea." The phooka was also blamed for causing blackberries to rot after Michaelmas, a Christian feast for Saint Michael the Archangel that took place every year in late September.[34]

"Puck" from Shakespeare's *A Midsummer Night's Dream*, as envisioned by Joshua Reynolds, 1789.

Jack-O'-Lantern

The Puck of English legend, by contrast, was "a jolly, frolicksome, night-loving rogue, full of archness, and fond of all kind of merry tricks."[35] The Welsh version, spelled pwca (pronounced "pooka"), was "a queer little figure, long and grotesque, and looked something like a chicken half out of his shell."[36] In the early 19th century, a man living in Cwm Pwca (Pooka's Valley), a secluded rural area in Clydach, Wales, told folklorist Thomas Croker the following story of an encounter with the Welsh puck:

"As he was one night returning home over the mountain from his work, he perceived at some distance before him a light, which seemed to proceed from a candle in a lanthern, and upon looking more attentively, he saw what he took to be a human figure carrying it, which he concluded to be one of his neighbours likewise returning from his work.

"As he perceived that the figure was going the same way with himself, he quickened his pace in order that he might overtake him, and have the benefit of his light to descend the steep and rocky path which led into the valley; but he rather wondered that such a short person as appeared to carry the lantern should be able to walk so fast.

"However, he redoubled his exertions, determined to come up with him; and although he had some misgivings that he was not going along the usual track, yet he thought that the man with the lantern must know better than himself, and he followed the direction taken by him without farther hesitation. Having, by dint of hard walking, overtaken him, he suddenly found himself on the brink of one of the tremendous precipices of Cwm Pwcca, down which another step would have carried him headlong into the roaring torrent beneath. And, to complete his consternation, at the very instant he stopped, the little fellow with the lantern made a spring right across the glen to the opposite side, and there, holding up the light above his head, turned round and uttered with all his might a loud and most malicious laugh; upon which he blew out his candle, and disappeared up the opposite hill."[37]

ROBIN GOODFELLOW

Robin Goodfellow is one of the oldest aliases, perhaps predating the jack-o'-lantern itself; his name has been found in manuscripts as far back as 1489.[38] Robin's history is a long and complicated one. He apparently started out not as a low-level imp or goblin, but as a much more threatening entity.

An English scholar writing in the sixteenth century, during the height of the witchcraft scare, said that the name of Robin Goodfellow had once evoked the same fear and terror among people as "hag" or "witch" did currently.[39] For reasons not completely understood, the name "Robin" – often seen as nothing more than a mild corruption of "Robert" – was often used to describe the Devil, as were other common monikers like Nick and Roger. Rather than try to find some deep etymological connection – which may or may not exist -- it seems more likely that the use of regular, everyday names was deliberate, a way of reinforcing the old Christian idea that the Devil was a master of disguises and often appeared in "sheep's clothing." In other words, the temptation to sin was everywhere around you, constantly, and even seemingly harmless words or actions could lead one to ruin.

A thirteenth-century collection of short stories describes a Robin-esque character ("Robinet") who made loud noises in the night to disturb a group of soldiers staying in a castle. When he finally stopped, one of the soldiers wondered aloud if they might be able to finally get some sleep. Robinet then replied, "I am not asleep, but am resting me, in order to shout the louder after." The anonymous writer summed up the moral of the story thusly: "So sinners sometimes abstain for a while from their wicked ways, in order that they may sin the more vigorously afterwards. The soldiers are the angels about Christ's body, Robin is the devil or the sinner."[40]

In the notorious *Saducimus Triumphatus*, a book on witchcraft written in 1681 by Joseph Glanvil, he recounts two instances where the name is used. In 1664, an accused witch named Elizabeth Styles

1639 illustration of Robin Goodfellow.

"confessed" that she had sold her soul to the Devil, and that "when she hath a desire to do harm, she calls the Spirit by the name of *Robin*, to whom when he appeareth, she useth these words, *O Satan give me my purpose*. She then tells him what she would have done." Another group of purported witches said that when they wanted to meet the Devil they would go to the forest at night and say "Robin" aloud, "upon which instantly appeared a little man in black clothes to whom all made obeisance, and the little man put his hand to his hat, saying, How do ye? speaking *low* but *big*."[41]

The combination of "Robin," with its sinister connotations, and the more optimistic "Goodfellow" points to the character's innate contradictions. At some point in the medieval era – no one is sure how or why -- the name's connection with Satan was more or less dropped and it became yet another term for the mischievous and friendly (at times, anyway) spirits that inhabited rural sections of Great Britain. In this new incarnation – let's call it Robin 2.0 – he was, like Puck, a trickster and shapeshifter par excellence. This excerpt from an old English poem describes him nicely:

Sometimes a cripple he would seem,
sometimes a soldier brave:
Sometimes a fox, sometimes a hare;
brave pastimes would he have.

Sometimes an owl he'd seem to be,
sometimes a skipping frog;
Sometimes a churn, in Irish shape,
to leap o'er mire or bog:

Sometime he'd counterfeit a voice,
and travelers call astray,
Sometimes a walking fire he'd be,
and lead them from their way.

Some call him Robin Good-fellow,
Hob goblin, or mad Crisp,
And some again do team him oft
by name of "Will the Wisp;"

But call him by what name you list,
I have studied on my pillow,
I think the best name he deserves
is Robin the Good Fellow.[42]

Two medieval representations of Robin Goodfellow in quasi-human form (one of many he assumed when he wasn't roaming around as a jack-o'-lantern). At left, Robin is a magician-like figure cloaked in moons and stars; at right, he is a hairy "wild man."

Robin 2.0 is also unique among jack-o'-lantern aliases for being partially human. According to legend, he was the child of a human mother and Oberon, a king of the faerie realm. Oberon visited the woman in her bed at night, and she never knew his identity; as one scholar pointed out, Oberon's behavior is disturbingly close to that of a classic incubus.[43] Here is the rest of Robin's origin story:

"By the time he was six years old he was so mischievous and unlucky that his mother found it necessary to promise him a whipping. He ran away and engaged with a tailor, from whom he also soon eloped. When tired he sat down and fell asleep, and in his sleep he had a vision of fairies; and when he awoke he found lying beside him a scroll, evidently left by his father, which, in verses written in letters of gold, informed him that he should have anything he wished for, and have also the power of turning himself 'To horse, to hog, to dog, to ape,' etc., but he was to harm none but knaves and [disreputable women], and was to 'love those that honest be, and help them in necessity.' He made trials of his power and found that he really possessed it. His first exploit was to turn himself into a horse, to punish a churlish clown, whom he induced to mount him, and gave him a fall that went well-nigh to break his neck. The fellow then went to ride him through a great [body] of water, and in the middle of it he found himself with nothing but a packsaddle between his legs, while Robin went off laughing, *Ho, ho, hoh*! He next exerted himself in the cause of two young lovers, and secured their happiness."[44]

Although often associated with the jack-o'-lantern, Robin Goodfellow was more accurately an alias of Puck. In *A Midsummer Night's Dream*, Act II, Scene I, we find this revealing exchange between a fairy and Puck:

FAIRY:
Either I mistake your shape and making quite,
Or else you are that shrewd and knavish sprite
Called Robin Goodfellow. Are not you he
That frights the maidens of the villagery,
Skim milk, and sometimes labour in the quern,
And bootless make the breathless housewife churn,
And sometime make the drink to bear no barm,
Mislead night-wanders, laughing at their harm?
Those that Hobgoblin call you, and sweet Puck,
You do their work, and they shall have good luck.

PUCK:
Thou speakest aright;
I am that merry wanderer of the night.
I jest to Oberon, and make him smile
When I a fat and bean-fed horse beguile,
Neighing in likeness of a filly foal;
And sometime lurk I in a gossip's bowl

In very likeness of a roasted crab,
And when she drinks, against her lips I bob
And on her withered dewlap pour the ale.
The wisest aunt, telling the saddest tale,
Sometime for three-foot stool mistaketh me;
Then slip I from her bum, down topples she,
And 'tailor' cries, and falls into a cough;
And then the whole quire hold their hips and laugh,
And waxen in their mirth, and neeze, and swear
A merrier hour was never wasted there.

This passage highlights some of Robin Goodfellow's unique characteristics. As the fairy notes, he was capable of both good and bad deeds. *The Mad Pranks and Merry Jests of Robin Goodfellow*, an English manuscript that dates back to at least the late sixteenth century (if not earlier), collected many Robin tales of the time period. He was known for visiting farmers' houses at night to help young maidens cook and do other household chores (typical behavior for domestic house spirits). In one story, he befriended a beautiful young woman and worked for six straight hours, accomplishing more than she could have in twice the time. The grateful girl wanted to do something for him in return. Noticing he wore no clothes, she sewed him a new waistcoat and left it out for him. Unfortunately, this wasn't proper faerie protocol; to keep Robin happy (and working), she was supposed to have left him milk or cream instead. When he returned the next night, he grew angry:

'Tis not your garments new or old
That Robin loves: I feel no cold.
Had you left me milk or cream,
You should have had a pleasing dream:
Because you left no drop or crumb,
Robin never more will come.

With that, he went away laughing "Ho, ho, hoh!" and the sad maiden was left to do all her own chores again.[45] Robin's laughter was an essential part of his character; in fact, in East Anglia in the 19th century, "to laugh like Robin Goodfellow" was a familiar saying that described "a long, loud, hearty horse-laugh."[46]

Another story from the same Elizabethan-era manuscript shows Robin Goodfellow engaging in typical jack-o'-lantern behavior. A group of young men were on their way home after a night of drinking and celebration. Robin intercepted them "in the shape of a walking fire" and "led them up and down the heath a whole night, so that they could not get out of it." At daybreak, he finally left them, saying:

Get you home, you merry lads:
Tell your mammies and your dads,
And all those that news desire,
How you saw a walking fire.
Wenches, that do smile and lips
Use to call me Willy Wispe.
If that you but weary be,
It is sport alone for me.
Away: unto your houses go
And I'll go laughing ho, ho, hoh![47]

Despite this puckish behavior, other tales present Robin Goodfellow in a positive, if not outright heroic, light. In one story, he comes across a man trying to rape a young maiden in a field. Robin quickly shapeshifts into a rabbit. He runs between the man's legs, then changes into a horse and carries the attacker away on his back, finally dumping him into a hedge filled with thorns that "left him so pricked and scratched, that he more desired a [salve] for his pain, then a wench for his pleasure."[48] By the early 19th century, after his popularity had waned, Robin was viewed much more warmly, and his previous indiscretions were mostly forgotten; in 1824, one writer classified him as belonging to "the order of white spirits."[49]

LANTERN MAN

The lantern man is a cantankerous, bad-tempered version of the jack-o'-lantern. It doesn't seek to mislead travelers out of a sense of playful mischief, but rather outright spite. In its plainest form, the lantern man (or men – they often travel in groups) is simply a more dangerous version of the mysterious nighttime lights.

In East Anglia, England, where it was particularly active, locals said that if you stood at the edge of a field and whistled, the lantern man would rush to meet the sound – and then try to kill you. People were warned not to provoke him, because he was apparently jealous of other lights illuminating the darkness. An old East Anglian fisherman said that he once attached a candle to the end of a pole and dangled it out his window to tease the lantern man, who had chased the man's friend earlier that night and given him a terrible fright. He waved the candle back and forth, and the goblin lunged at it several times, before finally catching it and tearing it to pieces. It was said that one way to protect yourself from the lantern man was to "throw yourself flat on your face and hold your breath."[50]

In East Norfolk, the resident lantern man "had the unpleasant habit of following the wayfarer home and lighting up his windows from the outside," wrote a Mr. Rye in 1872. "He is said to be awfully angry if you cross the meadows at night with a lantern. Once I heard of one following a man while he was carrying a lantern one night. The man knew what to do. He sat the lantern down and ran away as if the devil kicked him. When he ventured to look round there was the Lantern Man kicking the lantern over and over again."[51]

Unlike the jack-o'-lantern, which roamed across the fields with no sense of ownership, the lantern man sometimes claimed a particular patch of boggy ground or swamp and protected it from human interlopers. If you came near, it would "come for you," said an old East Anglian farmer named Ben. He recalled one night when a man ventured into the lantern man's territory with a lantern of his own, only to have the spirit "go right [through] him and take his breath right away."[52]

OLD HOB

Old Hob was another common name for the classic jack-o'-lantern floating through the nighttime fields of England. Variants include Hobany's Lantern, Hoberdy's Lantern, Hob and His Lantern, and other similar names.

Allies suggested that the name was a corruption of "Oberon's Lantern."[53] In medieval times, Oberon was a supernatural being and king of the faeries. However, Allies later noted several parallels with other folklore traditions. In Cheshire, England, the people had a tradition of dressing up a man carrying a horse's head and covered with a sheet. They called it Old Hob and it was meant to frighten people, at least in jest. The performance occurred sometime in the late fall or early winter. There were other equine clues: in Kent, townsfolk celebrated the "hodening" or "hobening," which involved carrying a horse's head during a Christmas Eve procession. All of these words likely derived from "hoppe," a word common in North German, Danish and Dutch dialects that means horse or mare. "As the movements of the [ignis fatuus] resemble in a measure the cantering motion of a horse, that may have bene the reason why the names in question were given to these interesting meteors," Allies wrote.[54] Ghostly horses were common in faerie mythology, and Robin Goodfellow often took the form of one to play his pranks or punish an evildoer.

Chapter 4

Jack-O'-Lanterns, Ghosts and Religion

As we've seen, the jack-o'-lantern and its varied forms had their beginnings in pagan faerie folklore. Eventually, however, a new branch of stories and legends began to grow and flourish during the Middle Ages in Great Britain and throughout Europe. This second category can be characterized as "Christianized" folklore, where the jack-o'-lantern and its aliases began to be viewed and processed through a prism of Christian beliefs mixed with a liberal dose of superstition. The old faerie stories were reframed and reinterpreted to reflect the dominant Christian dogmas of different regions and faiths. In their new form, these jack-o'-lantern stories also served as crude teaching tools – a way to reinforce the often rigid belief systems of both Catholics and Protestants among the common folk, especially in rural areas. These new jack-o'-lantern-type entities are sometimes associated with Christian saints (like the Sand Yan y Tad in Brittany), but many legends also portray them as being minions of the Devil (Robin Goodfellow in the previous chapter is a good example). Other incarnations, like the corpse candle and the death-fire, were seen as divinely inspired omens, warnings that someone was about to die. Others were viewed as pure ghosts or spirits of the dead.

This second category of jack-o'-lantern lore is much darker. The heavy-handed influence of organized religion resulted in a new set of didactic and often downright scary folk tales and superstitions.

A new breed of jack-o'-lantern aliases also emerged. Gone were the playful pranks of Puck and other imps and pixies. The mysterious lights no longer lured travelers off of country roads late at night; now they more often than not signified the tortured souls of dead sinners, frightening examples of what happens when one fails to follow the path of Christ (these stories were especially popular in parts of Germany and northern Europe). But there was a silver lining: by introducing the element of Western Christianity – and by forging a strong symbolic link between the jack-o'-lantern, death and the afterlife – this new set of stories also paved the way for the creation of modern Halloween, as well as the latest iteration of the jack-o'-lantern that has become such an indelible part of twenty-first century pop culture.

LOST SOULS

One of the most common "Christianized" explanations for the jack-o'-lantern was that each light represented the soul of a child who had died before being baptized, and thus was fated to forever wander the night alone, disembodied, unable to enter Heaven. This was probably the scariest advertisement ever developed for baptism, and the moral of the story was hard to miss: the sacraments of the church are important, so you'd better follow them…or else.

From the mid-19th century comes this story: "A Dutch parson, happening to go home to his village late one evening, fell in with three Will-o'-the-Wisps. Remembering them to be the souls of unbaptized children, he solemnly stretched out his hand, and pronounced the words of baptism over them. But, what was the consequence? A thousand and more of these apparitions suddenly made their appearance, evidently all wanting to be baptized. They frightened the good man so terribly, that he took to his heels, and made for home as fast as he could."[55]

In the old Lusatia region of central Europe (today parts of Germany and Poland), the local folklore was more optimistic: the

Jack-O'-Lantern

"wandering wildfires" were the souls of unbaptized children, but they were not harmful, and could be released from their predicament by throwing a handful of consecrated dirt at them.[56] A Netherlands tradition said that when the jack-o'-lanterns encounter a living soul, "they run up to him, and then hasten on before him, to show him the way to some water, that he may baptize them therewith. And that no one should neglect to do, because the poor beings must remain without the gates of paradise until someone takes pity on them."[57]

Jack-o'-lanterns could also represent the dead in general. One of the more disturbing tales comes from Rathenow in north-central Germany. A farmer, returning from tending his cows, noticed that one was missing. He went looking for her in the forest until it grew dark. Exhausted, he sat down on a tree stump and took out his pipe. Out of nowhere, a "countless multitude" of jack-o'-lan-

David Acord

Shutterstock

terns appeared "dancing wildly" around him. He remained calm and continued preparing his pipe. The jack-o'-lanterns grew even more aggressive and began to fly around his head. The farmer got fed up, grabbed a stick and started swinging at them. Every time he hit one, more appeared. Finally, he reached out and grabbed a jack-o'-lantern in mid-air (one of the few times in all the folklore that someone actually manages to catch one, by the way). But when he opened his hand to examine it, all he found was a human bone. Instantly, the other jack-o'-lanterns disappeared. He put the bone in his pocket and went home. The next night, he was sitting at home when he saw lights outside the window. He went to investigate and saw that the entire street was filled with jack-o'-lanterns. "If you don't give us our comrade, we will burn your house!" they cried. He scoffed and told them the bone couldn't possibly be one of them, but they repeated their threat even more loudly. Finally, he held the bone outside the front window of his house. It immediately turned into a jack-o'-lantern and flew away, along with the others.[58]

A similar story, from the village of Storkow in northern Germany, told of a clergyman driving home in his carriage late one night with his servant when they saw the familiar lights moving toward them. Then the lights began to multiply, and soon there were so many that the horses became frightened and refused to move. The clergyman began to pray aloud, but this only succeeded in attracting even more jack-o'-lanterns. Finally, the servant told his master, "Just leave that off...I'll send them packing," and yelled "Will ye be off in the devil's name!" The lights immediately disappeared.[59]

A tradition from Normandy, France explained that the light, known as a *feux follet*, was the spirit of a woman who had had an affair with a church minister and was therefore doomed to run through the night aflame.[60] Another belief said it was the soul of a priest who had broken his vow of chastity and was forced to wander in eternal exile.[61] Both were heavy-handed ways of reinforcing the importance of hewing to a religious moral code. In England, a Catholic superstition held that the lights (especially those seen in churchyards and cemeteries) were souls that had broken out of purgatory to pray for deliverance. At least one writer claimed this belief was encouraged by the clergy so that parishioners would give them money to say mass for the lights, "everyone thinking it might be the soul of his or her deceased relations."[62]

In Denmark, jack-o'-lanterns were known as *Lygtemaend*, or Light-men, and were thought to be "spirits of unjust men" seeking to waylay innocent travelers[63] or "lunatics unable to rest in their graves" – though in the latter case, they might be persuaded to guide a traveler in the right direction if he or she tosses a small coin to them.[64] A story from Stulpe, Germany in the mid-1800s told of an old man who always relied on the light-men to see him home safely in bad weather. He would summon them by simply calling out, "Come, and light me home!" He would leave a half-penny outside his door as payment, and in the morning it would always be gone.[65]

When dealing with less friendly jack-o'-lanterns, villagers were warned not to point at them, because the lights viewed this as an invitation to come near. Another way to protect oneself if accosted by a jack-o'-lantern was to remove your cap and turn it inside out.[66] A resident will-o'-the-wisp in Normandy would chase after anyone who ran away from it; the only way to escape was to throw oneself face-down on the ground and call out to God for help.[67]

In Neatishead, a village in the English county of Norfolk, a jack-o'-lantern constantly vexed the residents throughout the eighteenth century. It was said to be the soul of a man who had committed "unmentionable crimes" and had drowned in the nearby swamp. "I have seen it there," a longtime resident of the village recalled in the 1840s, "rising up and falling, and twistering about, and then up again. It looked exactly like a candle in a lantern."[68] She added, "If anyone were walking along the road with a lantern, at the time when he appeared, and did not put out the light immediately, Jack would come against it and dash it to pieces; and...a gentleman, who made a mock of him and called him Will of the Wisp, was riding on horseback one evening in the adjoining parish of Horning, when he came at him and knocked him off his horse." She also recalled a story her father told, of the jack-o'-lantern following him home one night after an old man he was traveling with "whistled and jeered" at the light; it proceeded to terrorize them when they arrived home, hovering around the windows. On another occasion, a group of night travelers attempted to get rid of the jack-o'-lantern by reading aloud portions of Bible scripture, but it responded by reciting the next verse before they could. Finally, a young boy laid a pair of pigeons in front of the light, which for some reason confused the spirit, and they were able to banish it.

Sometimes the lights took on quasi-human form. Nineteenth-century author Carl Engel relates the following legend from Germany: "On the ridge of the high Rhon, near Bischofsheim, where there are now two morasses [i.e., bogs], known as the red and the black morass, there stood formerly two villages, which sunk into the earth on account of the dissolute life led by the inhabitants. There appear on those morasses at night maidens in the shape of dazzling apparitions of light. They float and flutter over the site of their former home; but they are now less frequently seen than in the olden time. A good many years ago, two or three of these fiery maidens came occasionally to the village of Wustersachsen, and mingled with the dancers at wakes. They sang with inexpressible sweetness; but they never remained beyond midnight. When their allowed time had elapsed, there always came flying a white dove, which they followed. Then they went to the mountain, singing, and soon vanished out of sight of the people who followed, watching them with curiosity."[69]

One of the most common post-pagan explanations for jack-o'-lanterns – perhaps even more widespread than the unbaptized children theory – was that they represented the tortured souls of dishonest landowners. In rural farming cultures, one of the worst things you could do was steal land from a neighbor by secretly moving the stones that marked the boundary between properties. This excerpt from an 1881 monograph captures many of the fascinating details:

"A popular belief in Sweden says that 'Jack-with-the-Lantern' was formerly a mover of landmarks, and for his unjust acts is doomed to wander backwards and forwards, with a light in his hand, as if he were in search of something. Thus, he who in his lifetime has been guilty of such a crime is believed to have no peace or rest in his grave after death, but to rise every midnight, and with a lantern in his hand to proceed to the spot where in days gone by the landmark had stood which he had fraudulently removed. On reaching the place, however, he is seized...with the same desire which instigated him in his lifetime when he went forth to remove his neighbor's landmark, and he says as he goes, in a harsh voice: 'It is right! It is right! It is right!' But on his returning, qualms of conscience and anguish seize him, and he then exclaims: 'It is wrong! It is wrong! It is wrong!' There is also a Danish tradition which informs us, that near Skovby, on the isle of Falster, there are many Jack-o'-Lanterns. They are believed to be the souls of land-measurers, who, having in their lifetime perpetuated injustice in their measurements, are doomed to run up [to] Skovby [and back] at midnight, which they measure with red hot irons, exclaiming, 'Here is the clear and right boundary! From here to there.'"[70]

Many superstitions also held that the jack-o'-lantern, in various forms, was an omen of impending death or general misfortune. One of those species was "the wat," a ghostly light that haunted Aylesbury Gaol, a prison in Buckinghamshire, England. The night before the judges were to arrive to hear criminal cases, a small flame would appear, and it was "considered fatal to every prisoner to whom it became visible."[71] This general belief wasn't limited to the criminal class; 18th-century Italian peasants also believed that if a person found him or herself constantly followed by jack-o'-lanterns, it meant they would soon die, and so they came up with the name "death-fires."[72] Another alias, the elf-candle, was also thought to be a bad omen for anyone who saw it.

In Denmark, ghostly sparks were sometimes seen when carpenters were building a house. The sparks, which manifested whenever a worker put a saw or axe to a piece of wood, were omens that the house would one day be consumed in a fire. Such a phenomenon was called *forbrand*, or "burning beforehand." The Danish clergyman H.R. Feilberg collected many firsthand accounts of *forbrand* in the late 19th century. In some instances, people would see a house or field engulfed in flame and go running to help, only to discover it was all an illusion. There was a rich folklore tradition concerning fire omens in Denmark, especially in rural areas. Most structures were made of wood, therefore fire was the ultimate destroyer, and in pre-industrial days little could be done to stop a conflagration once it started. As a result, a bevy of superstitions arose that both soothed and stoked fears. Certain people were even said to be endowed with a mysterious power and could "put away" the fire after it had been foretold, moving it into a rock or even a body of water where it remained safely imprisoned.[73]

CORPSE CANDLES

When it comes to mysterious lights acting as omens, though, the most widespread myth throughout Great Britain and Europe was that of the corpse candle, also known as the dead man's candle. This linkage between the jack-o'-lantern and death was perhaps inevitable. As discussed earlier, the lights were often seen in wet, marshy areas and produced by decaying organic matter. During the medieval era and up through the 19th century, graveyards in England and Europe were often extremely primitive, and burial practices were shockingly crude by modern standards, especially in remote rural communities. More often than not, bodies were buried in nothing but simple cloth shrouds; coffins were optional and usually too expensive for hand-to-mouth farmers to afford. Cemeteries were established next to local churches with little thought as to whether or not the terrain was suitable for interring bodies, so many burials occurred in low-lying areas with poor drainage. To make matters worse, corpses were often placed very close to one another and put in shallow graves just a few feet deep. This set of circumstances created a "perfect storm" – the decaying and putrefying corpses produced methane, which seeped up through the ground and often manifested as strange flickering lights at night (see the discussion on the scientific basis of the jack-o'-lantern in Chapter Two).

In a morbid twist, these mismanaged cemeteries became hot spots for tourists looking to catch a glimpse of the mysterious lights. T.L. Phipson, writing in London's *Belgravia* magazine in 1868, shared with readers a long list of his personal favorite locations for viewing the jack-o'-lantern. "But of all the places where Will-o'-the-wisp may be seen in its full splendor," he wrote, "there are none with which I am acquainted that equal in this respect to the churchyard outside the town of Gibraltar [in Buckhinghamshire]. This locality has been known for some years as a very remarkable spot on many accounts, and the climate appears to be extremely favorable to the development of *ignis fatuus*. The soil of the cemetery is very sandy; many of the graves are not more than three feet deep; if it is attempted to dig them deeper the earth falls in. Burials are very frequent and space very scarce. Though no flames are observed in the daytime, the putrid odor which arises from the soil is more easily imagined than described. In fact, it is a locality *par excellence* for Will-o'-the-wisp, and we recommend it to the attention of lovers of natural philosophy."[74]

As its name implies, the appearance of a corpse candle was thought to presage death. Like other Christianized incarnations of the jack-o'-lantern, the corpse candle was seen as a true supernatural presence from beyond the grave, and its existence was confirmed (and even promoted) by many ministers and church officials. Indeed, some of the greatest folklorists of the 18th and 19th century were members of the British and European clergy, who collected countless ghost stories and tales of weird encounters from their parishioners. Edmund Jones, an English reverend who recorded numerous corpse candle accounts, defended his rather morbid hobby this way:

"But some may yet enquire what may be the end and design of amassing together accounts of this nature, and making them public? ...In answer to this, I avow that it is designed to prevent a kind of Infidelity which seems to spread much in the kingdom, especially among the Gentry and Nobility, even the denial of the being of Spirits and Apparitions, which hath a tendency to irreligion and atheism; for when men come to deny the being of Spirits, the next step is to deny the being of God who is a Spirit, and the Father of Spirits...Also the Scripture of truth both the Old and New Testament speaks of the Apparitions of Spirits both good and bad; and if they appeared in times past, why not in times present and future?"[75]

The legends surrounding the corpse candle are many and varied. Sometimes it appeared as a regular jack-o'-lantern, with its light resembling that of a candle, while in other instances it took the form of a spectral human being – or parts of one, anyway. In the small town of Sommerda in Germany, it appeared not as a candle, but as a lantern held only by a severed floating hand. At night, it would follow departing travelers to the edge of town and disappear once they passed through its gates.[76]

In Wales, it was known as the *Canwyll gorf*, a kind of ghostly doppelganger; the apparition took on the appearance of an actual living person and walked alone at night, glowing softly and carrying a candle. This meant that the person would soon die. Usually a passerby who knew the person would see it and inform them of their impending demise. The glow of the *Canwyll gorf* also varied according to gender; the male version shone more brightly, while the female version emanated "a pale and delicate blue light."[77]

The corpse candle legend was widespread throughout Wales in the 18th and 19th centuries – perhaps more popular there than in any other region of Great Britain or Europe. The Rev. John Price, a Welsh clergyman, tried to explain the legend's persistence. Writing in 1895, he noted that pre-Christian peoples buried their dead at night, and while Christians only conducted burials during the day, they still carried candles – perhaps a holdover from the pagan era. The candles were easily explained as being the Christian symbols of "life, illumination, joy and happiness." Price also wrote, "In Wales, in quite recent years, lighted candles were placed near the body of the deceased, and kept burning day and night, while a pewter plate containing salt was placed on the breast of the deceased to keep away the evil spirits. Now what more natural when a light was seen in the vicinity of a house where someone was ill, or seen on the road between the house and the burial place, than that as an imaginative people should come to the conclusion that the light was associated with death and a funeral, and yet withal with a happy release?"[78]

There were many Welsh beliefs associated with the corpse candle. It was said to be a divine manifestation of St. David, a sixth-century Welsh bishop. As Sabine Baring-Gould explained in 1905, the bishop "promised that no Welshmen in his territory should die without the premonitory sign of a light travelling to his house from the churchyard to summon him. In the Cambrian Register for 1796 we read of 'A very commonly received opinion, that within the diocese of S. David's, a short space before death, a light is seen proceeding from the house, and sometimes, as has been asserted, from the very bed where the sick person lies, and pursues its way to the church where he or she is to be interred, precisely in the same track in which the funeral is afterwards to follow.'"[79]

Baring-Gould also shed some light on why such a morbid tale took hold among the Welsh: "Funerals are a vastly popular institution in Wales, and everyone in the district is expected to attend. When a peasant dies the first consideration is to provide a sufficient number of candles, as the corpse must be sat up with all night; also the making and baking of a great soul-cake, to be eaten on the day before the interment, when crowds visit the house of mourning to have a last look at the dead person, and to descant on his or her virtues."[80]

The Welsh corpse candle was pugnacious – it would often strike at people and knock them unconscious (though, in fairness, they often tended to deserve it, at least according to the prevailing morals of the day; young men walking home drunk after a night of debauchery were common victims). "Many of the old folks profess to have seen it; one of them related that his grandfather saw it while walking on the road late in the evening," noted the historian M.J. Walhouse. "On coming near he uttered a friendly greeting, thinking it was a wayfarer, but saw, to his amazement, that the light came from a lantern held by a hand only. He was one of the 'common-sense people,' who scouted the supernatural and would not believe the evidence of his eyes, so he struck with his stick at the light, and was instantly hurled with terrible force to the ground, where he lay for a time senseless; on coming to himself he could not find his way, and only reached his home after midnight. So in Wales, anyone rashly interfering with or attempting to stop a corpse-candle was struck down and stunned. It is ill jesting with these appearances."[81]

Edmund Jones collected many valuable firsthand accounts from Wales in the early 19th century. Joshua Coslet, a resident of Llandeilo Fawr, a small village in southwestern Wales, told him of encountering a corpse candle in the more traditional jack-o'-lantern form of a small light that grew larger as it moved away from him. "He could easily perceive that there was some dark shadow passing along with the candle," Jones wrote, "but he was afraid to look earnestly upon it… He also said that some dark shadow of a man carried the candle, holding it between his three forefingers over against his face." Later on, a funeral processional passed by the same spot where he saw the light. Jones noted that "others have seen the likeness of a candle carried in a skull,"[82] a tantalizing detail that may have influenced the development of the modern jack-o'-lantern, as the "face" carved into the pumpkin resembles a rudimentary skull. But we're getting ahead of ourselves.

In another account published by Jones, a man from the Welsh parish of Llanboidy told of glimpsing a corpse candle one night on his walk home. He decided to investigate and moved in closer – never a good decision when dealing with corpse candles. He discovered the light was actually a ghostly burial procession, and the corpse "was the perfect resemblance of a woman in the neighborhood whom he knew, holding the candle between her forefingers, who dreadfully grinned at him; and presently he was struck down from his horse, where he remained a while, and was ill a long time before he recovered. This was before the real burying of the woman. His fault, and therefore his danger, was his coming presumptuously against the candle."[83] Some hardy souls figured out a workaround: if they saw a corpse candle, they would hide by the side of the road for a better look. As long as they didn't approach or disturb it, they were left alone and allowed to watch the ghostly procession.[84]

A Welshman named John Davis, writing in 1656, outlined his

countrymen's surprisingly elaborate belief system concerning corpse candles. The lights "mark out the way for corpses...sometimes before the parties themselves fall sick, and sometimes in their sickness," he explained in a letter to Richard Baxter, a popular English Puritan theologian of the time. Small, pale candles giving off a bluish light represented the death of an infant or stillborn child; larger lights signaled an adult would soon die; and multiple corpse candles meant that the same number of people would die together, most likely in an accident of some sort. Two candles seen moving toward one another from opposite directions meant that two people from different regions would die and be buried at the same time.[85] The speed at which the light moved was also a clue: a fast-moving light meant that a child or younger person would die soon, while a slow-moving corpse candle indicated the imminent death of an older person.[86]

The route the corpse candle followed, as well as the precise the nature of its movements along that route, were also important, because they "mapped out" either how someone would die or the particular circumstances of how the corpse would be moved to the cemetery. Davis told the story of a group of neighbors who saw a corpse candle moving up and down along the riverbank. A few weeks later, a young woman tried to cross the river in the exact same place the light was seen. The neighbors warned her not to, as the waters were high due to recent rains. Frustrated, she walked back and forth along the riverbank, her movements mimicking exactly those of the corpse candle weeks earlier. Eventually she tried to cross and was drowned.[87]

Victorian novelist Catherine Crowe, in her nonfiction exploration of ghostly phenomena *The Night-side of Nature* (1848) – a huge bestseller in its day – told of a woman from Aberystwith, Wales who was traveling at night on horseback to visit a friend. Halfway there, she stopped to wait for her friend's house-servant, who would guide her the rest of the way. While waiting, she encountered a light moving toward her about three feet off the ground. Suddenly it stopped in the middle of the road and remained there, motionless, for almost half an hour before moving on. The house-servant showed up a little after that and took her on to her friend's house. A few days later, that same servant fell ill and died. His body was carried along the same road, "and, at the very spot where the light had paused, an accident occurred, which caused a delay of half an hour."

Crowe also related the following story: "A servant in the family of Lady Davis, my informant's aunt, had occasion to start early to market. Being in the kitchen, about three o'clock in the morning, taking his breakfast alone, when everybody else was in bed, he was surprised at hearing a sound of heavy feet on the stairs above; and, opening the door to see who it could be, he was struck with alarm at perceiving a great light, much brighter than could have been shed by a candle, at the same time that he heard a violent thump, as if some very heavy body had hit the clock, which stood on the landing. Aware of the nature of the light, the man did not await its further descent, but rushed out of the house...As his mistress, Lady Davis, was at that period in her bed, ill, he made no doubt that her death impended; and when he returned from the market at night, his first question was, whether she was yet alive; and though he was informed she was better, he declared his conviction that she would die, alleging as his reason what he had seen in the morning...The lady, however, recovered; but, within a fortnight, another member of the family died; and as his coffin was brought down the stairs, the bearers ran it violently against the clock – upon which the man instantly exclaimed, "That is the very noise I heard!" [88]

The Dying Light

Beliefs linking corpse candles or jack-o'-lanterns to impending death weren't limited to England and Europe. Cultures around the world have long considered the appearance of unexplained lights to be dire omens. For instance, Native American tribes in New England, as well as the Inuit peoples in the Arctic regions, believed that lights seen above the roof of a dwelling indicated someone living there would soon die.[89] From 19th-century Scotland comes this anecdote: "A girl died in Kintyre, and on the morning of her death, an hour or two after the event, her brother came into the house and reported that he had seen a strange, bright light passing over his head, outside the house, which rose up and disappeared at about the height of the upper lintel of the door. One present remarked that 'it was she,' referring to the girl who had just died."[90]

But where does this primal connection between light and death come from? "Light and heat are naturally associated in the mind, and warmth and life," Dr. R.C. Maclagan theorized in 1897. "Thus, when life leaves the body its heat departs, and what more natural than to suppose that the visible source of heat, light, should be evident at the same conjuncture?"[91]

Many accomplished 19th-century physicians testified to having witnessed lights appear above patients' bodies shortly before they expired, and attributed them to chemical reactions signaling the initial stages of decomposition. "That the body becomes luminous after death under certain circumstances is well known to most medical men whose pursuits have connected them much with the dissecting room," noted one writer in 1848. He related the story of Dr. Hart, who said, "Having had occasion to enter the dissecting room of the Park Street School of Medicine on a dark, damp night in 1827, my attention was attracted by a remarkably luminous appearance of the subjects on the tables, similar to that which fishes and other marine animals exhibit in the dark. The degree of illumination was sufficient to render the forms of the bodies, as well as those of muscles and other dissected parts, almost as distinct as in the daylight. This luminosity was communicated to my fingers from contact with the dead bodies, from any part of which it could be removed by scraping it, or wiping it with a towel. I observed that the surfaces of the dissected muscles were brighter than any other parts."[92]

Another doctor in the same time period related this incident about a female patient named Louisa (or L.A.) that he was treating: "It was ten days previous to L.A.'s death that I first observed a very extraordinary light which seemed darting about the face and illuminating all around her head, flashing very like an aurora borealis. She was in a deep decline, and had that day been seized with suffocation, which teased her much for an hour, and made her so nervous that she would not suffer me to leave her for a moment, that I might raise her up quickly in case of a return of this painful sensation. After she settled for the night...this luminous presence suddenly commenced. Her maid was sitting up beside the bed, and I whispered to her to shade the light, as it would awaken Louisa. She told me the light was perfectly shaded. I then said, 'What can this light be which is flashing in Miss Louisa's face?'"

"The maid looked very mysterious, and informed me she had seen that light before, and it was from no candle. I then inquired where she had perceived it; she said that morning, and it had dazzled her eyes, but she had said nothing about it, as ladies always considered servants as superstitious...[The light] was more silvery, like the reflection of moonlight on water. I watched it for more than an hour, when it disappeared. It gave the face the look of being painted white and highly glazed, but it danced about and had a very extraordinary effect. Three nights after, the maid being ill, I sat up all night, and again I saw this luminous appearance when there was no candle, nor moon, nor, in fact, any visible means of producing it. Her sister came into the room and saw it also. The evening before L.A. died I saw the light again, but it was fainter, and lasted but about twenty minutes."[93]

Even a doctor as well-respected as Sir Henry Marsh, President of the King and Queen's College of Physicians in Ireland, had an encounter with the "death lights." In 1842, he began treating a young lady in the final stage of pulmonary consumption. Her brother gave Marsh the following eyewitness statement: "About an hour and a half before my sister's death, we were struck by a luminous appearance proceeding from her head in a diagonal direction. She was at the time in a half-recumbent position, and perfectly tranquil. The light was pale as the moon, but quite evident to mamma, myself, and sister, who were watching over her at the time. One of us at first thought it was lightning, till shortly after we fancied we perceived a sort of tremulous glimmer playing round the head of the bed; and then recollecting we had read something of a similar nature having been observed previous to dissolution, we had candles brought into the room, fearing our dear sister would perceive it, and that it might disturb the tranquility of her last moments."[94] Marsh speculated that such a phenomenon might account for the "halo effect" often seen in paintings of martyred saints. Had they emitted a similar light before they died?

Sir Walter Scott, in a footnote to one of his poems in which he mentioned a corpse candle, claimed that a man who had drowned in a river was eventually discovered because the lights were seen hovering over his submerged body.[95] The famed 19th-century German scientist Baron von Reichenbach studied "highly sensitive" patients with apparent parapsychological powers. He took one of these subjects, a young woman named Rachel, to cemeteries at night, where she was able to see lights hovering over certain graves– lights that were invisible to others. "She described the appearance less as a clear flame than as a dense vaporous mass of fire, intermediate between fog and flame," he wrote. "On many graves the flame was four feet high, so that when she stood on them it surrounded her up to the neck. If she thrust her hand into it, it was like putting it into a dense fiery cloud."[96]

Others theorized that if light emanated from a dying body, it was possible for that light to become "stamped" with the outline of that body – in other words, the light took on the appearance of the person. Another word for this spectral, glowing entity would be a ghost.[97]

Taking Things Literally

Among 19th-century criminals and the underclass, the corpse candle wasn't just a legend. In 1889, the *London Standard* reported that four thieves in Kursk, Russia had murdered a young girl "in order to make candles of her body." They believed that the resulting (and literal) corpse candles would render them invisible during a forthcoming robbery they intended to commit. "In the German criminal codes of the seventeenth and 18th centuries...and also in statutes of a more recent date," the *Standard* report added, "there are express penalties against a crime, the motive of which was the making of... 'thieves' candles,' or 'sleep-producing candles,' one of the ideas being not only that such a light enabled the person carrying it to be unseen by his victim, but...it will also throw the victim into the deepest slumber."[98]

A related belief – and only slightly less gruesome – was that of the "dead man's hand." The folklore among criminals was that if you brought along the severed hand of a dead man on your next robbery and placed a candle in it, the thieves would turn invisible and the residents of the house would not wake until after they had left. Sometimes the phrase, "Let those who are asleep be asleep, and let those who are awake be awake," was whispered while moving the hand and candle around the house. Baring-Gould relates this tale: "Two magicians having come to lodge in a public-house with a view to robbing it, asked permission to pass the night by the fire, and obtained it. When the house was quiet, the servant-girl, suspecting mischief, crept downstairs and looked through the keyhole. She saw the men open a sack, and take out a dry withered hand. They anointed the fingers with some unguent, and lighted them. Each finger flamed, but the thumb they could not light; that was because one of the household was not asleep. The girl hastened to her master, but found it impossible to arouse him. She tried every other sleeper, but could not break the charmed sleep. At last, stealing down into the kitchen, while the thieves were busy over her master's strong box, she secured the hand, blew out the flames, and at once the whole household was aroused."[99]

The dead man's hand was also known as the "Hand of Glory." Colin de Planey, in his *Infernal Dictionary* (1818), gave this description and recipe: "The Hand of Glory is the hand of a man who has been hung, and is prepared in the following manner: Wrap the hand in a piece of winding-sheet, drawing it tight so as to squeeze out the little blood which may remain; then place it in an earthenware vessel with saltpeter, salt, and long pepper, all carefully and thoroughly powdered. Let it remain a fortnight in this pickle till it is well dried, then expose it to the sun in the dog-days til it is completely parched, or, if the sun be not powerful enough, dry it in an oven heated with vervain and fern. Next make a candle with the fat of a hung man, virgin wax, and Lapland sesame. The Hand of Glory is used to hold this candle when it is lighted. Wherever one goes with this contrivance those it approaches are rendered incapable of motion as though they were dead."[100]

Bizarrely, the dead man's hand was also thought to have miraculous healing powers. In the seventeenth century, "the hand of an executed man readily fetched ten guineas, being held as efficacious in working cures as the holy bones of the saintliest of saints,' wrote Prof. James Mackintosh in 1879. "Hangmen added to their income by taking money from persons desirous of receiving the dead-stroke; and it is still an article of popular faith in some parts of England, that a swollen neck may be reduced to its normal proportions by simply striking it three times with the hand of a man who has been hanged, but the operation ought to be performed before the criminal is cut down."[101]

In 1830, an English newspaper reported, "The execution at Lincoln of the three men who were condemned to death…drew an immense concourse of people…Two foolish women came forward to rub the dead men's hands over some [cysts] or diseased parts of their bodies, and one of them brought a child for the same purpose."[102] These beliefs probably have something to do with the folklore surrounding the hand in general. Since ancient times it has been a symbol of power, "as the wielder of scepter, sword and, and pen should be, [it] is the symbol of authority the world over."[103]

Jack-O'-Lantern

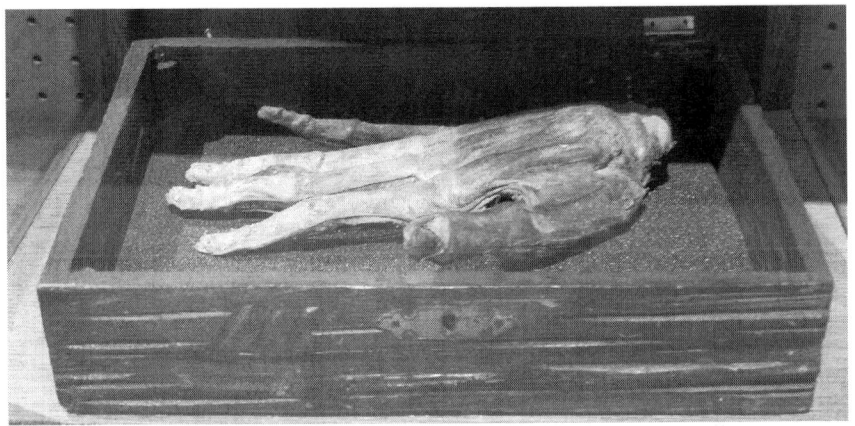

A 19th-century "hand of glory" on display at the Whitby Museum, UK. Photo credit: www.badobadop.co.uk

TREASURE LIGHTS

Jack-o'-lanterns were also sometimes called "treasure lights" or "mineral lights" and were thought to indicate the presence of buried treasure. H.F. Feilberg wrote in 1895, "They are seen burning on many a hill on the ancient sites of castles, or on ruins. It is commonly said that where a light burns something is hidden – perhaps an evil deed, perhaps a treasure... A farmer, returning one night from a visit, discovered a light burning and knew at once that a treasure must there be hidden. So, being more clever than others, he hastened home to get the necessary working tools. Without speaking a word or answering a question, he returned with these to the wood, where he again found the place of the burning light and began digging, while a couple of ravens made a dreadful noise. And the deeper he dug the more turbulent the ravens became; and when his spade at last pushed against a trunk the ravens attacked him, striking him with their wings, till he exclaimed in terror: 'Christ be gracious to me, they are going to crush my head!' Instantly the trunk disappeared, and the ravens desisting from their importunity took flight to a neighboring tree, where they sat croaking: 'Now you may seek the treasure in another wood.'"[104]

SEA LIGHTS

Encounters with strange lights weren't restricted to forests and rural areas. For centuries, sailors reported seeing a wide variety of luminous objects in oceans around the world. Sometimes they used familiar names to describe them – jack-o'-lanterns and corpse candles being the most common. The seventeenth-century English writer John Fryer, who saw the lights during a storm, dubbed them the *"ignis fatui* of the watery elements."[105] But because the sea lights often exhibited different characteristics than their landlocked cousins, soon a new maritime-specific folklore began to emerge.

The most common lights were those seen at the tops of ships' masts during or just before a storm. When the electrically charged atmosphere came into contact with the mast, the air around it was ionized and a static discharge occurred, creating glowing, colored plasma lights; sometimes a hissing sound was also heard. Unlike the classic jack-o'-lantern of the English countryside, this type of meteorological phenomenon is not only readily explainable, but is still common today, occurring not just on ships but airplane wings, the spires of tall buildings and many other structures. In the proper atmospheric conditions, static charges can also produce lights on fingertips, hair and the fur of animals.

A shipmaster related the following encounter at sea in 1830: "After several days of stormy weather, one evening about 8 p.m. during a light shower, which had been preceded by a hail-squall, a jack-o-lantern was seen on the maintop-gallant masthead, and an intelligent person was sent up to examine it. He found it formed by a circle of lights round the masthead, eight or ten in number, and one or two inches apart. Each flame was about two inches long, was where it

Jack-O'-Lantern

joined the head about the size of a knitting needle, and the extremity larger than the flame of a candle, and nearly as bright, of a pale blue color, each making a noise similar to steam out of green wood, while burning; no smell was susceptible. Upon striking it with the hand the lights were extinguished, and small sparks adhered to the hand for a moment, then disappeared. In a few seconds, the lights again began to burn; after several blows they entirely disappeared."[106]

The sea lights predate the land-bound jack-o'-lantern by many centuries. We find several references to them in ancient Greek literature. A single light seen above a ship was known as "helene," Greek for "torch" – this was often softened to "Helena," giving the lights a feminine nature. In Greek mythology, Helena (also known as Helen of Troy) was the beautiful daughter of Zeus. Because she was often depicted as the "cause" of the Trojan War, Helen wasn't held in the highest repute; thus, seeing a single light bearing her name was considered bad luck. However, if two lights were seen above the mast, it was interpreted as good luck. These twin lights were called Castor and Pollux, after the brothers from Greek myth. They were also children of Zeus and thus Helena's brothers. Castor and Pollux were sometimes referred to as the Dioskouri, Greek for "sons of Zeus," and the lights were often called that as well. According to myth, Castor and Pollux were Argonauts who accompanied the hero Jason on his quest to find the golden fleece. As they were sailing, they ran into a storm, and lights appeared above both the brothers' heads, which the poet Orpheus interpreted as a sign of protection from the gods.

In the first century A.D., Roman scholar Pliny the Elder wrote, "I have seen, during the night-watches of the soldiers, a luminous appearance, like a star, attached to the javelins on the ramparts. They also settle on the yard-arms and other parts of ships while sailing, producing a kind of vocal sound, like that of birds flitting about. When they occur singly, they are mischievous, so as even to sink the vessel, and if they strike on the lower part of the hull, setting them on fire. When there are two of them, they are considered auspicious, and are thought to predict a prosperous voyage, and it is said they drive away the dreadful and terrific meteor named Helena. On this account their efficacy is ascribed to Castor and Pollux, and they are invoked as Gods." Euripides, Horace, Lucian, Maximus of Tyre and other writers and poets of the classical era also reference the lights in their writings.

Like the jack-o'-lantern, the sea lights eventually became "Christianized." By the time of Columbus, they were frequently called St. Elmo's fire, named after the third-century saint who, after his death, became the patron saint of sailors; he was also known as Saint Erasmus. Speaking of Columbus – the great explorer actually saw the lights on his second voyage to America, writing: "On Saturday, at night, the body of St. Elmo was seen, with seven lighted candles in the round top, and there followed mighty rain and frightful thunder. I mean the lights were seen which the seamen affirm to be the body of St. Elmo, and they sang litanies and prayers to him, looking upon it as most certain that in these storms, when he appears, there can be no danger."[107] In 1598, the English writer Richard Hakluyt saw the lights during an ocean storm and they remained aboard the ship, "flying from mast to mast," for several hours.

The Spanish and Portugese called the lights the "corpo santo," or "holy body," believing they represented the presence of a saint; in both instances, the lights were seen as signs that the sailors were under divine protection. Over the centuries, sailors associated the lights with many other saints as well. "In the history of the voyage of Magellan there is mention of the appearance of three brilliant lights on the masts of the ship, which instantly quelled a storm," a 1907 encyclopedia noted. "The sailors called them the three heavenly bodies, St. Anselmo, St. Ursula and St. Clare. Fournier, a writer of the 17th century, relates many curious stories of this light. It was named, he says, after a saint, familiarly known as Saint Telme, but who was San Pedro Gonzales de Tuy, in Galicia, who had been a mariner, then was canonized, and became a patron saint of sailors. Galician sailors called the light San Pedro Gonzales. The phenomenon also has been known by the name of St. Hermes, St. Ermyn, St. Helen, St. Nicholas, St. Peter, St. Anne, or, indeed, by that of any one of a hundred other saints...Another writer says [the lights were named after] a Sicilian bishop, who, when at sea in a storm, was taken very ill. He promised the distressed mariners, in dying, that he would appear if they were destined to be saved. After his death a light appeared at the mast head and was named for him."[108]

But as with rural lights in the countryside, the sea lights were sometimes seen as bad omens or associated with death. Scottish sailors called the lights "sea-fire," "water-fire" or "water-burn." An early 18th-century belief on the Isle of Man was that lights seen over water predicted a drowning; the lights were also thought to hover over drowned bodies. A similar legend sprung up around the River Dee in Wales; it was thought that whenever someone drowned in the river, the spectral lights would float above the water to aid in the recovery of the body. This phenomenon was known as the Holy Dee.

Both German and American sailors believed the light was the spirit of a sailor who had died on board ship; the Americans called it "Ampizant." Fletcher Bassett related many other legends regarding the sea lights as well. In Greece they were known as "telonia," a word he deciphers as meaning "primarily, a demon tax-gatherer, from an old Christian superstition that demons hindered souls, in their heavenward journey, to gather toll. Hence, this light is a bad omen. It breaks masts, destroys ships and crew; and hence, prayer and incense are used against it. Incantations from the *Clavicle of Solomon* [a medieval Italian magical grimoire] are said, a loud noise is made, and guns fired. If a pig is on board, its tail is pulled, as its diabolical cries will expel the demon."[109]

David Acord

Part Two

Creating the Modern Jack-O'-Lantern

David Acord

Chapter 5

Jack and the Turnip

Of all the Christianized tales involving the jack-o'-lantern, none has been more pivotal and influential than the story of a man named Jack and his encounter with the Devil. In this legend we find the seeds not only for the modern incarnation of the jack-o'-lantern but also the eventual connection it would share with Halloween.

The roots of the Jack tale stretch back at least to the medieval era in Europe and probably much earlier. There are literally hundreds of variations found the world over, but a few commonalities emerge regardless of the plot details: Jack is almost always portrayed as a ne'er-do-well and someone not to be trusted – usually a farmer or blacksmith with a bad reputation. But he is also a highly clever and mischievous man capable of frightening and/or fooling the Devil himself, at least for a little while. In other words, Jack is a trickster *par excellence*. In addition, a glowing lantern of some sort is present, usually carried by Jack at the end of the story after his fate is sealed (thus, "jack-o'-lantern"). It's an open question whether the Jack legend was created to explain (and give a name to) the mysterious lights that wandered across the European countryside in the first place, or if it was later coopted due to coincidental similarities.

There are many stories of how Jack came to carry his "lantern." A popular 18th-century English folktale told of a fellow named Jack who was well known for his rude behavior. However, one day he takes pity on an old beggar and allows him to stay at his house and share his dinner table. The next morning, the beggar reveals that he is, in fact, an angel (or, in some versions, St. Peter himself), and as a reward for being so nice, gives Jack three wishes. However, Jack wastes his wishes on meting out petty revenge against his neighbors, and the exasperated angel bans him from ever entering Heaven. Twenty years later, the Devil shows up at Jack's door; he knows that Jack is barred from Heaven and has come to collect his soul. However, Jack is such a miserable human being that he actually frightens the Devil and runs him off. When Jack finally dies, the Devil, still afraid, refuses to allow him into Hell; instead, he takes a burning coal from the underworld, tosses it into a hollow turnip, and sentences Jack's spirit to forever wander through the world of the living, a soul without a home, with only the coal to warm him and light his way.

In other versions of the story, Jack, after living a wasted life of sloth, laziness and endless carousing, is about to die. The Devil comes for his soul, but after a bit of back-and-forth, they make a bargain, usually to extend his life for a certain period of time. But clever Jack finds a way to temporarily weasel out of his agreement, sometimes by nailing the Devil to a chair, other times by convincing "Old Nick" (as Satan was known back then) to transform himself into a pile of coins, which Jack quickly places into a purse pouch emblazoned with a crucifix, trapping the beast inside. The Devil eventually escapes, only to be thwarted twice more -- three times is always the charm in these stories. Finally, Jack is defeated. He dies, but his soul is barred from both Hell and Heaven, and he wanders the night aimlessly, with only a lantern to guide him and help him trick travelers into wandering off the main roads; Jack is still a jerk, and deceiving the living is the only joy he has left. The source of the light inside Jack's lantern varies. Sometimes, as in the first story above, it's a chunk of coal from Hell; other times the light is Jack's own soul, or a glowing ember from his blacksmith's forge that he carries with a pair of tongs.

Importantly, many of the Jack stories describe the lantern that holds the light as a carved turnip, not a pumpkin. Pumpkins were a

Jack-O'-Lantern

New World plant and rare in Great Britain and Europe at the time. For centuries, several types of hollowed-out turnips – including the rutabaga and the mangel-wurzel, a large, yellowish variety – were used as lanterns by farmers and rural folk in England, Scotland and Ireland. Sometimes large beets and even potatoes were utilized instead. These makeshift light sources served a variety of practical, decorative and superstitious purposes. Vegetables were plentiful on farms, so the lanterns were relatively cheap and easy to make: simply cut a hole in the top, core out the vegetable material, stick a candle inside, and thread a string or wire through it to carry it. Oftentimes the lanterns were tied to long sticks rather than carried by hand – it was safer that way and lowered the risk of burning

A boy and his turnips: an example of the popularity of turnip lanterns in the Victorian era. "Making Lanterns" by Edward Docker, late 19th c.

David Acord

your fingers while you made your way through the night. Or, you could simply set the lantern on a table or ledge to illuminate your work (of course, it needs to be pointed out that carving large vegetables or gourds for both practical and ceremonial reasons was by no means limited to Western cultures; the practice dates back thousands of years and can be found on several continents, including Africa).

Inevitably, turnip lanterns – also known as turmit-lanterns and bob-a-lanterns – were put to mischievous use. An 1889 glos-

"Affrighted Travelers, or the Illumined Turnip," late 18th-century illustration. An example of how the turnip lantern was used by pranksters to scare travellers at night -- but not specifically as part of Halloween celebrations.

sary defined a turnip lantern as "a large turnip, hollowed out, with mouth, eyes and nose made in it to imitate the human face. A candle is put inside and it is used by silly persons for the purpose of affrighting people simpler than themselves."[110] Jabez Allies, the father of 19th-century jack-o'-lantern research, recalled, "In my juvenile days I remember to have seen peasant boys make, what they call a 'Hoberdy's Lantern,' by hollowing out a turnip and cutting eyes, nose and mouth therein, in the true moon-like style; and having lighted it up by inserting the stump of a candle, they used to place it upon a hedge to frighten unwary travelers in the night."[111] In South Cheshire, England in the late 1800s, the turnip lantern was, according to one researcher of the period, "a common device of mischievous lads for frightening belated wayfarers on the road – the popular idea of 'Owd Scrat' [Old Scratch, another name for the Devil], with eyes of fire and breathing flame, being pretty accurately represented by one of these hideous turmit-lanterns."[112]

Not surprisingly, turnip lanterns were popular with young children, who would often carve faces or other decorations into the sides (this also helped with ventilation and ensured the flame received a steady supply of oxygen). However, unlike the modern pumpkin jack-o'-lantern, it was customary not to carve all the way through the turnip, but to keep the thin skin intact. Here is how one Irish author instructed his young readers to make a turnip lantern in 1873:

> "...First, procure as large a turnip as possible, and then proceed with your pocket knife to scrape out all the substance of the turnip, leaving only the rind or skin. You will find this takes no small pains and patience, care being required not to penetrate the rind, as this would let the wind in and blow out the candle. Having scraped all the substance out of your turnip, and made a hole in the lid to let out the smoke, proceed to cut on the outside a man's face...Do not cut the

shell of the turnip quite through but cut as thin as possible, so that as much light and as little wind may get through as possible. Thus the light portions of the face will shine out against the darker and thicker parts of the skin. You must make a hole in the bottom of the lantern to receive the candle. When this is lighted all is complete, and you may now call on some of your friends and show your lantern. Let this, of course, be done at night, and on as dark and quiet a night as possible. But what I consider the crowning success of a 'turnip lantern' is, to place it some dark night on the top of a pillar of snow. It is then that your man's face will show to advantage, and doubtless a little astonish any who may happen to pass by."[113]

It's important to note that the tradition of carving faces into these turnip lanterns originally had nothing to do with Halloween; however, it was only a matter of time before the connection was made. In one sense it was inevitable, like the merging of two companies with complementary product lines. Halloween, after all, was a time for playing tricks, and when the barrier between our world and the supernatural temporarily disappeared; what better way to celebrate than by trying to scare passersby with a lantern that resembled a demon or other monster?

So when did turnip lanterns become associated with Halloween? It's difficult to pinpoint an exact date or "smoking gun" event where the two came together, because neither exist. Like most cultural changes or shifts in folk tradition and belief, it likely happened in a gradual, nonlinear fashion, starting in small villages and counties and eventually spreading across Great Britain (and, later, to America). However, using a couple of primary sources, we can state with a fair degree of accuracy that the carved turnip lantern – predecessor to the modern jack-o'-lantern – became an integral part of Halloween sometime between the late eighteenth and mid-nine-

Jack-O'-Lantern

*Irish turnip jack-o'-lantern, early 20th century.
Photo credit:
rannpáirtí anaitnid*

*Modern turnip lantern.
Photo credit: Geni.*

teenth century, at least in Scotland. How do we know this? First, we take a look at "Halloween," a poem written in 1785 by the great Scottish bard Robert Burns. The long poem details a Halloween celebration in rural Scotland, and is brimming with details about the customs of the holiday – it's a virtual Scottish Halloween encyclopedia. Interestingly, despite the poem's specificity and length, neither turnip lanterns nor jack-o'-lanterns are mentioned even once. Their absence is striking, and lends weight to the theory that they were not yet an important part of the holiday in that region.

For the second source, we jump ahead to a *New York Times* article dated October 31, 1866. It describes a Halloween parade in Scotland where boys "form themselves into long processions, each bearing hollowed turnips with devices marked on the shell and illuminated by candles..." So, somewhere between Burns' poem and the *Times* article, the turnip lanterns grew popular enough to be included in Halloween parades.

By the 1890s, turnip lanterns were a common Halloween fixture on both sides of the Atlantic – although curiously, they were still not referred to as "jack-o'-lanterns" (that seems to have been reserved for their pumpkin cousins). An account of how Scottish children celebrated Halloween in 1895 noted their prevalence. "These turnips have the features of a wild human face cut out and accentuated in the rind so that the candle placed within may give light through eyes, nostril and mouth. The lid fits tightly and is painted to represent shaggy, wild locks, whilst blue and red paint marks off cheeks, etc., all adding to the general weirdness, even gruesomeness, of this moving humanlike head. When a band of ten or twenty 'guisers' [children in costume] fantastically dressed carry these grinning lights aloft the effect on weaker minds is, to say the least, terrifying. Strong minds even may begin by admiring the wild, picturesque effect, but too often end by experiencing a cold shiver in the region of the backbone."[114] Meanwhile, a large and elaborate Halloween party in Chicago in 1894 featured "whole

Jack-O'-Lantern

rows of turnip lanterns with gorgeous colored paper eyes, mouth, and nose effects, emphasized by a light behind. These grotesque glowing masks were strung on all sides of the spacious barn, beaming down with broad and fiery grins on the assembled guests."[115]

Turnip lanterns also played a role in the spiritual lives of rural folk. Carved lanterns were set on windowsills to ward off evil spirits[116], and in the Baden region of Germany, they were placed on graves of relatives on All Saints Day and All Souls Day (November 1 and 2, respectively) along with flowers and other decorations. Inscriptions, rather than human faces, were carved on the turnips, and "if any child steals a turnip lantern or anything else from a grave, the indignant ghost who has been robbed appears to the thief the same night and reclaims his stolen property."[117]

Modern turnip lantern from Cornwall, England.

Chapter 6

The Jack-O'-Lantern Comes to America

After hundreds of years in Europe and Great Britain, the jack-o'-lantern finally crossed the Atlantic and came to America with the first colonial settlers in New England. However, a second and far larger wave of immigrants, primarily from Scotland and Ireland, made their way to the United States in the late eighteenth and nineteenth centuries and brought with them a much wider and deeper pool of shared folklore and superstition than their Puritan forebears. These millions of new citizens are the ones who really helped popularize the jack-o'-lantern in their new homeland. With their newfound Yankee ingenuity, they also quickly transformed it into the present incarnation so familiar to us today. Almost as soon as the jack-o'-lantern legend arrived in America it began to change... and what's more American than that?

As we have discussed, the jack-o'-lantern began its life as a mysterious light flitting through moonlit fields, luring British and European travelers and farmers off the main roads and into swamps. However, with the advent of new farming and drainage techniques – not to mention the advent of industrialization -- much of the original jack-o'-lantern's boggy habitat was wiped out by the mid-nineteenth century. This destruction coincided with a gradual transformation of the legend. Since it was no longer seen in the wild, it was eventually "brought indoors," so to speak, and domesticated. It gained an outer shell, usually in the form of a carved turnip, with the light

Jack-O'-Lantern

Harper's Weekly, 1867.

David Acord

Popular illustration, c. 1872.

nestled inside. Over time its definition changed so that "jack-o'-lantern" referred simultaneously to both the light and its vegetable carrying case. The various legends surrounding the protean trickster character of Jack helped to reinforce this new image, as he wandered the earth after his death carrying a glowing turnip lantern.

In this new form, rather than spending its nights trying to trick someone into stumbling into a lagoon or briar patch, the jack-o'-lantern instead began serving as a prop in Halloween celebrations and other late-fall/early-winter festivities. It also became a common part of a rural home's décor, usually propped on a windowsill or shelf.

Jack-O'-Lantern

Women show off their jack-o'-lanterns, U.S. c. early 1900s.

The housewife who placed it there probably knew very little about its pre-turnip history, or the fact that the softly glowing light was once thought to be the soul of an unbaptized baby. Instead, the jack-o'-lantern became a vaguely supernatural symbol, one that was inviting and even comforting. Its carved face looked primitive, and brought back nostalgic memories of scary ghost stories heard as children in the days before kerosene lanterns and railroads. It was also a symbol of innocent childhood and wholesome (for the most part, anyway) pranks played at Halloween. *This* was the jack-o'-lantern tradition English and Scotch-Irish immigrants brought with them to America.

And when they arrived, they found a pleasant surprise: pumpkins. Lots and lots of pumpkins – cheap, easy to grow and hardy. Technically a fruit, this colorful member of the squash family was

David Acord

U.S. postcard linking Thanksgiving with the jack-o'-lantern, c. early 1900s.

native to North America and came in a dizzying array of varieties, all carefully cultivated by Native Americans over the centuries, even millennia, as an important food source (archaeologists have found domesticated seeds for the common orange "field pumpkin" in Mexico dating back 10,000 years[118]). Americans first discovered the sweet possibilities of pumpkin pie in the late eighteenth century, and the pumpkin's popularity began to grow. It quickly became an integral part of early American culture, promoting the idea of wholesome, rural farm life. Due to the fact that pumpkins grew quickly and were often produced in great quantities, it also became tied into notions of the bounty, abundance and promise of this new land. There were more than enough pumpkins to go around – and more than enough freedom and opportunity, provided you worked hard enough.

But immigrants quickly discovered another great thing about the fruit: it was big, soft and easy to carve, much easier than turnips and beets. The pumpkin made the perfect jack-o'-lantern. The first references to the pumpkin jack-o'-lantern in America in literature date to the early nineteenth century. Instructions for making them were common, especially in books and periodicals for children (carving jack-o'-lanterns was, from the very beginning, considered a juvenile activity). However, these early references say almost nothing about Halloween; making jack-o'-lanterns – either for decorative purposes or to play tricks and frighten neighbors at night – was still largely separate from the fall holiday.

The November Connection

In some areas of the country, jack-o'-lanterns came to be associated with Thanksgiving before, or along with, Halloween. This makes sense, as pumpkins are harvested in late fall and thus still plentiful right around the November holiday. Consider this 1899 children's poem, "Out for A Walk," by L.F. Armitage, which fuses the sinister, trickster nature of the jack-o'-lantern with warm-and-fuzzy Thanksgiving sentiments:

OUT FOR A WALK

Jack-o'-Lantern went for a walk
With a turkey gobbler gay
The time they chose for their promenade
Was the night of Thanksgiving Day.

Said the Jack-o'-Lantern, "Let us go
And into the window peep,
Where Billy Boy, tired out at last,

David Acord

Is lying fast asleep.

On tiptoe, then, up the hill they stole,
"We'll frighten him well," said they,
"Then he'll not want to eat all our brothers up
On next Thanksgiving Day."

"Gobble, gobble," then cried the gobbler gay,
And Billy woke at the sound.
He sat up in bed and rubbed his eyes,
And began to look around.

But when he saw the grinning face,
And the bird with bristling wings,
He thought of witches and brownies and imps,
And all those kinds of things.

And he gave a scream and hid his face,
And his mother soon was near.
"What is the matter, my son?" she said.
"You are feeling ill, I fear."

"They are after me! They are after me!"
Cried Billy with streaming eye;
"You are dreaming," his mother said.
"You've had too much turkey and pumpkin pie."

But the Jack-o'-Lantern grinned with glee,
And whispered, "Now come away,
We'll stay out all night and find all the boys
Who've eaten too much today."[119]

Jack-O'-Lantern

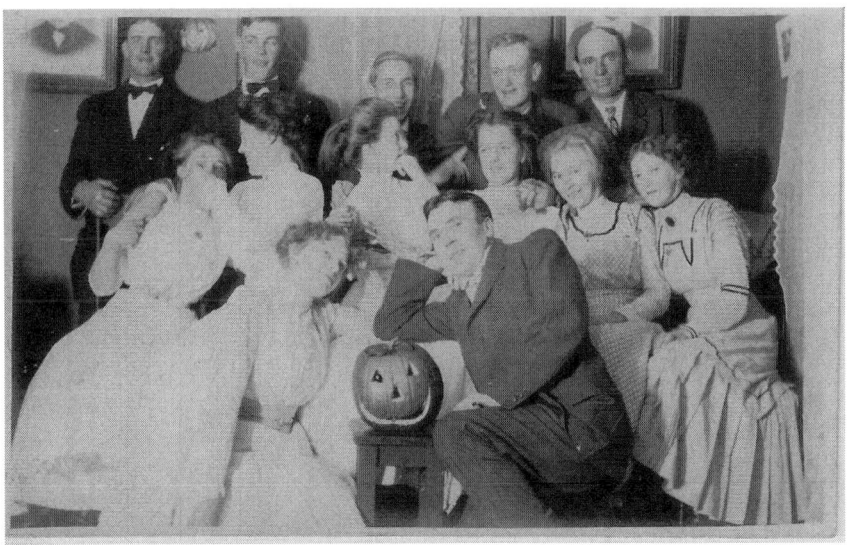

Jack-o'-lantern takes center stage at a Halloween party, U.S., c. early 1900s.

There are also numerous references to "Thanksgiving jack-o'-lanterns" in American newspapers in the late nineteenth and early twentieth centuries. In a 1905 piece titled "Thanksgiving Signs," one writer waxed eloquently, "The Jack O'Lantern is in the window...the pumpkins – a golden store – are piled high in the dooryard, the cranberries have been raked from the bogs, and the turkeys are fattening on their autumn menu, acquiring a fine plumpness and delicacy of flavor for the Thanksgiving market. The earth has given bountifully of its increase and while still the tang of its varied fruits is in the air it is meet that thanks be offered to Him Who ordains seed-time and harvest."[120]

A children's story from 1914 told of a family of early Puritans in New England who were attacked by Indians at Thanksgiving time while their father was gone. They set a jack-o'-lantern in the window to frighten off the attackers, and when the father returned, he declared, "We must always have a Jack o' Lantern at our Thanks-

giving feast." The mother replied, "Yes, and we are truly grateful to the good God for sparing our lives, for he guided the children to use their Jack o' Lantern for our protection."[121] The ironic part about the jack-o'-lantern being framed as a wholesome, even Christian part of Thanksgiving is that its true origin – one of pagan tricksters, banished souls and the like – was the exact opposite of the values celebrated at the holiday: healthy crops, bountiful harvests, love and abundance, the new values of a relatively new and hopeful country.

Remember, Remember...

The jack-o'-lantern was also connected to another historical celebration, this one having to do with revolution and treason. Guy Fawkes was a member of a group of English Catholic conspirators

Jack-O'-Lantern

Pumpkin carving, c. early 1900s.

Facing page: early Halloween trick-or-treaters with jack-o'-lantern.

who plotted to assassinate King James I (a Protestant) by blowing up the House of Lords in London on November 5, 1605. The plan was foiled when Fawkes was caught guarding a large cache of gunpowder in a hidden room underneath the building – thus the name "Gunpowder Plot" was born. He was swiftly executed along with several other conspirators, many of whom were hanged, drawn and quartered; some even had their heads displayed on pikes. The next year, the English Parliament declared November 5 a national holiday, and the defeat of the conspirators was celebrated by lighting huge bonfires, shooting off fireworks and ringing church bells. People wore grotesque masks imitating Fawkes, and effigies of him were burned

Group of female friends with jack-o'-lantern, early 1900s.

as well; the holiday came to be known (informally) as Guy Fawkes Day, or the "British Fourth of July," and was also an excuse for revelers to engage in rabid anti-Catholic sentiment. A famous nursery rhyme became synonymous with the celebrations: "Remember, remember/ The Fifth of November / Gunpowder treason and plot; / For I see no reason / Why Gunpowder Treason / Should ever be forgot."

Because Guy Fawkes Day was held in close proximity to Halloween celebrations, many of the same traditions and activities overlapped. It was common for children to create crude effigies of Fawkes that would later be burned on community bonfires; they would parade the effigies in the streets beforehand and beg for money to buy fireworks, similar to the "a-souling" common during the Halloween season and a direct precursor to the American custom of trick-or-treating. Jack-o'-lanterns were also a part of many Guy Fawkes Day festivities, both in England and early colonial America. In fact, use of pumpkin jack-o'-lanterns in American Fawkes

Jack-O'-Lantern

celebrations amy have influenced their use on Halloween as well. "From the earliest colonial times in New England," wrote one historian, "the custom having been brought over by the first settlers, the fifth of November was celebrated by burning an effigy of Guy Fawkes and by letting off fireworks, or by carrying about the village street at night a pair of hideous 'pumpkin faces' with candle-ends inside. These were supposed to represent the Pope and the devil, and they were burned together in a fire on the common."[122]

The similarities between the two holidays is illustrated in this excerpt from a newspaper in Portsmouth, New Hampshire in 1892. It describes activities on Guy Fawkes Day, but they could easily have been mistaken for Halloween antics: "The celebration of the anniversary of Guy Fawkes' night on Saturday by the young people of this city was not so extensive as in former years, no doubt owing to the conditions of the streets, but nevertheless

Woman with jack-o'-lantern, c. early 1900s.

small bands paraded the streets and made the early part of the evening hideous with music from the tin horns they carried for the occasion. Some carried the usual pumpkin lanterns. The ringing of door-bells was also extensively indulged in. Very few of the paraders knew that the celebration was in keeping of the old English custom of observing the anniversary of the discovery of the famous gunpowder plot to blow up the House of Commons."

From 1867 comes this fascinating account of early customs involving pumpkins and Guy Fawkes Day. Originally published in *Harper's Weekly*, it is worth reprinting at length:

> Many of the quaint old customs prevalent in New England a few years ago are now almost forgotten... Among the minor sports now but seldom practiced

Halloween party with jack-o'-lantern centerpiece, 1923

Jack-O'-Lantern

by the urchins of the country is that...of "The Pumpkin Effigy"...The sport of the pastime consists in paring a pumpkin to resemble a human head, and placing a light within to illuminate it, suddenly expose the monster thus created to the view of passing persons, frequently to the very considerable horror of more youthful and more timid persons. The pastime came to this country from England, whence we naturally derive, with our blood and language, many others of our customs. The Fifth of November — "Guy Fawkes's Day" — is annually observed in England with something like this custom as it prevails here, though the effigies, which are called "Guy Fawkeses," are made of turnips instead of pumpkins, and being placed on a long stick, and attired in a long coat, are paraded about the streets. The "pumpkin effigies" as used in this country had no particular design, as those of England, and no other purpose than amusement, the writer of this can remember an instance in which the use of one produced much terror and pain.

"Pumpkin effigies" were little known in the South fifteen years ago, and the first appearance of one in the little country town in which the writer resided was, owing to certain unfortunate circumstances, long remembered and talked of. It was known that what was there called a "gang of negroes"—literally a chain gang of slaves on their way further South—were to pass through the town that evening, and a number of mischievous urchins prepared a "pumpkin effigy," with which to frighten them and amuse themselves. The negroes had never seen such an object, and when it was suddenly displayed as they were passing they were panic stricken, and fled in great fright. As they were handcuffed together at the wrist-men, women, and children alike—and united by a strong chain which ran the whole length of the file, they soon became confused in their flight, and the weaker ones were thrown to the ground and much bruised and injured. Their overseers, or "drivers" as they were called, on securing them, abused and maltreated them still further. "Pumpkin effigies" became thereafter very unpopular in that region of the South; but few seemed to think the originator of the evil was the individual who had thus bound the helpless creatures together.[123]

A Perfect Match

By the late 1800s, despite some lingering connections to Thanksgiving and other ancillary celebrations, a new link had been firmly established between the pumpkin jack-o'-lantern and Halloween. While there was no historical connection between the two, in hindsight the union was only a matter of time. The parallels were too striking to ignore. Halloween was a season of tricks and pranks, and the jack-o'-lantern had its origins in tricking nighttime travelers off of roads; Halloween took place in late fall, a time when the traditional jack-o'-lantern of old (a roaming, disembodied light) was most often witnessed, and when pumpkins were most plentiful; turnip jack-o'-lanterns had been used to scare passersby for decades, and Halloween emphasized scares and spooks of all kinds. There was also the largely subliminal connection between Halloween's origins as a pagan celebration where the borders between our world and the supernatural realm of the dead disappeared for the night, and the various old superstitions that connected the jack-o'-lantern to ghosts and lost or banished souls (unbaptized children, dishonest farmers and property landlords, unchaste women, etc.).

Jack-O'-Lantern

Passing down a tradition through three generations: grandfather shows grandchildren how to carve pumpkins while father looks on, early 1900s. This photo perfectly represents the American idealism that attached to the idea of the jack-o'-lantern: it represented family, childhood, tradition, nostalgia, and all the warm hearth-and-home sentiments of rural life.

Pumpkins had also been a part of Halloween celebrations in early America before they were used as jack-o'-lanterns. It was common for youngsters to steal pumpkins and other vegetables from farmers' gardens, then place them on doorsteps or sidewalks so that adults would trip over them in the dark. In addition, the pumpkin already had a somewhat spooky pedigree; it featured prominently in Washington Irving's wildly popular short story "The Legend of Sleepy Hollow," published in 1820. One night, traveling home from an autumn harvest party, the unlucky schoolteacher Ichabod Crane had a frightening encounter with a mysterious supernatural horseman who carried his severed head on his saddle. The next morning, Crane was gone, and all that was left was a small sack containing his belongings, as well as a shattered pumpkin. Irving subtly implies that Crane's romantic rival, Brom Bones, impersonated the horseman and frightened off Crane by throwing the pumpkin at him – and Crane, thinking it was his head, either died of fright or ran away, never to be seen again. Over the years, many people have mistakenly claimed that the pumpkin had been carved into a jack-o'-lantern (a Disney animated adaptation of the story in 1946 helped to spread that belief), but in fact, that term is never used in the story; Irving specifically describes a "shattered pumpkin," and nothing more. It was just a normal pumpkin that may (or may not) have served as the head for a fearsome ghost.

Unfortunately, there is no historical "smoking gun," no documented instance where someone in authority said, "Hey, I know – let's start using the jack-o'-lantern at Halloween!" and it snow-

Pumpkin carvers, U.S., 1917.

Univesrity of Southern California student Halloween party, 1890.

balled from there. There is no secret memo outlining the strategy for integrating the two. That's not how traditions work – or change. As I mentioned earlier in this chapter, when discussing the first transformation of the jack-o'-lantern from a loose ball of light to something held inside a turnip, there is no linear path to trace back; for the various reasons I listed above, the merging of the jack-o'-lantern pumpkin with Halloween "just happened," much like viral memes take hold today on Facebook or Twitter – first here, then there, and then, suddenly, everywhere.

David Acord

New American Legends & Traditions

When the jack-o'-lantern legends first reached America, they began to transform and multiply, just as they had in England and Europe for hundreds of years prior. Many settlers were surprised to find that the same phenomenon of ghostly lights existed in their new homeland. Just as their ancestors had created stories to explain these wandering sprites in the Middle Ages, the new arrivals began to do the same in New England, Pennsylvania and across the Midwest and South.

American jack-o'-lanterns were commonly referred to as "spook lights," "ghost lights," "swamp fire" and similar names. Many rural areas of the country apparently had environmental conditions similar to Great Britain centuries earlier, when jack-o'-lantern sightings

Children placing jack-o'-lanterns around home for Halloween, U.S. c. 1919.

Jack-O'-Lantern

Children with jack-o'-lanterns, U.S., c. 1930s.

were most common. Once again, bogs and swamps were prime real estate for the strange lights, especially (though not exclusively) in cold weather. John Hicks, a former schoolteacher in the remote Ozark mountains of Arkansas, recalled a "cold, drizzly October night in 1925" when he walked outside to take a break after grading papers:

"Peering through the fog, I saw what appeared to be a lighted lantern among the willows. At first I thought it was someone gigging frogs [in the nearby pond]; then it occurred to me that frogs were in hibernation. My second look revealed three globular, bluish-white lights about the size of basketballs bobbing about over the surface of the water. These eerie objects maneuvered the pond for several minutes and disappeared among the willows. Standing there – alone – in the midnight silence, watching these mysterious lights drifting about like fireflies in the darkness, I had the sensation of treading on unholy ground."

Hicks went on to recall an earlier jack-o'-lantern sighting in the same area when he was a child. His grandfather was with him at the time and told him, "Now, those little old lights are not going to hurt you one little bit. During the [Civil War] while I was down South in the swamp country, we saw them nearly every night. The folks down there call them swamp fire or mineral lights and think if you follow one it will lead you to a gold mine or a lost treasure. But, of course, that is superstitious nonsense."[124]

The following newspaper article from early 1890 shows just how ingrained in American culture these strange lights had become by the late nineteenth century:

A JACK-O'-LANTERN TOWN

GHOSTLY GLIMMERINGS IN THE LACKAWANNA VALLEY.

STRANGE NIGHT SCENES IN THE TOWN OF ARCHBALD –
GOOD MATERIAL FOR GHOST STORIES.

SCRANTON, Penn., Jan. 18 – Have you ever heard of the "moving lights" of the Lackawanna Valley? They present an interesting phase of a phenomenon which has exerted a strange influence over the minds of many persons in the mining hamlets of Northeastern Pennsylvania, and particularly in and about the village of Archbald, which stands a little to the north of midway between Scranton and Carbondale. The mere mention of "the lights" to any resident of Archbald is sufficient to convey the significant meaning which usually attaches in that neighbor-

Jack-O'-Lantern

hood to the mysterious midnight glimmerings that are frequently seen hovering over the shallow river that runs through the town, drifting along the mountain side or floating over the tops of the houses.

These mystic lights have been seen at all hours of the night by persons who firmly believe that they are manifested by ghostly hands. A certain old lady who has frequently seen the "lights" solemnly avers that at various times she has observed a candle held by a spectral hand, and carried swiftly along the mountainside and over the housetops in the dead of night. That she saw the light there can be no doubt whatever, but the hand was furnished by her imagination – that is certain.

These lights have been seen most frequently emerging from the mouth of an old, abandoned colliery called the Sebastopol Mine, where it is said several persons met a violent death several years ago. Others have seen them dancing across the village graveyard, and others yet at the dilapidated water wheel. It is needless to say that these particular landmarks have been regarded with no small degree of awe for years past, but the terror is not so great now as it was ten or fifteen years ago, when the "lights" were usually spoken of with bated breath by those who actually believed that they were manipulated by the spooks and hobgoblins, who took a sort of fiendish delight in frightening the poor mortality that were not well versed in the scientific causes from which such phenomena proceed.

The "oldest inhabitants" could of course tell some hair-raising stories concerning the ghostly lights and the thrilling experiences of the pioneers who encountered them. Among the stories current of bygone days, or rather nights, when these haunting lights were first observed, is one of a mysterious glimmer that actually spoke to one of the "old settlers" on his way home from the upper end of the village. Of course it was past the midnight hour, "when churchyards yawn," and the hero of the adventure, Phil Crehan by name, was returning from a raffle with a fine fat turkey he had won under his arm. Just as Mr. Crehan was passing the "Bottomless Mine" a light started up from the mouth of the shaft, and after hovering about for a few seconds, as if undecided as to the course it should take, it flickered merrily to his side. Phil Crehan was a man of powerful physique and rare cour-

Jack-O'-Lantern

age, but he confessed afterward that when he saw the uncanny light keeping him company for a hundred rods or so, it made him feel rather shaky. This was nothing, however, until the light began to talk to him.

"You are out rather late, Phil, for a man of family," it began. Thinking silence was golden under the circumstances, Mr. Crehan made no reply, but hastened forward. As he did so, the light darted ahead of him, and with a laugh, which he described as a "light laugh," it said: "Oh, not so fast, Phil, I am not so easily left behind. I see you had good luck at the raffle," said the light rather sarcastically, and as it spoke it fastened itself to the head of Mr. Crehan's turkey, giving the gobbler the quaint appearance of having an illuminated head.

By this time Phil plucked up some courage, and he replied, with a slight show of temper: "Well, what if I did? I don't see that it's any of your business."

"It wouldn't be if you played fair," retorted the light, "but you know you won the turkey by cheating, and if you attempt to eat the bird it will choke you."

Mr. Crehan knew that his playing had not been entirely fair, but it startled him to think that this flickering, intangible thing with a voice should be aware of his conduct. The threat of choking so terrified him that he actually lost his appetite for turkey. In his desperation he blew at the offending light with all his power of lung, hoping to extinguish it, but the result was that instead of going out, as he intended it should, the tiny light burst into a great sheet of flame, which entirely enveloped the turkey, and Mr. Crehan in his terror flung away the blazing bird and ran home as fast as he could. Instantly the light disappeared, leaving the darkness more intense than ever, and there was a loud peal of mocking laughter which echoed all along the mountains.

When next Phil Crehan met the men who were interested with him at the raffle he noticed that they grinned rather suspiciously when they asked him how he enjoyed his turkey, but he did not care about investigating the matter any further, as his recollection of his experience with the spooky light was anything but pleasant.

A more recent and serious episode of the uncanny lights is one that for a considerable length of time made the life of a sober, industrious young man most unhappy. It was his custom in the evenings, after his day's work, to visit a young lady living on the outskirts of the village, to whom he was engaged. Every night on his way home at a certain point, a faint blue light would start up beside his path and keep him company the greater portion of the way. The light would change at times from a blue to a deep red flame and then it would become white. At first the young man was much terrified by the apparition, and even after he had heard it scientifically explained he could not bring himself to think that it was anything less than supernatural. He could not shake off the feeling that he was haunted, and this made his wife so miserable that he finally moved away to a town thirty miles distant. Since then he has not, of course, been annoyed by the haunting light which made his life so miserable during his stay in Archbald.

The queer lights have been seen by scores of others, and a good many believe that they are carried about by spooks and hobgoblins. Those who made a study of the movements of the luminous visitors noticed that they were frequently observed moving from a lonely spot where a man was found dead, to a dilapidated shanty in which a poor woman was burned to death some years ago. Another favorite spot for the lights was around the haunted dwelling in which a widow was found dead in her bed. Other equally gruesome scenes are mentioned, including the bottomless shaft in which a party of men were drowned long ago, and which is situated at the foot of an abrupt slope called Dutch Hill.

The mystery of the haunting lights is easily explained. They are nothing more nor less than the old-fashioned will-o'-the-wisp, sometimes spoken of as the *ignus fatuus*. They arise from the gases generated in the old mines, where the decaying timber of the props and other prolific causes contribute to their existence. Rising out of the mines at night and floating about like tiny comets, they present a strange study and are well calculated to strike fear to the stoutest heart. The town of Archbald is probably not more subject to these luminous visitors than other mining towns, but its sheltered situation between two hills gives it special opportunities for studying the phenomenon that has given rise to many a ghost story and weird tradition.

David Acord

The term "spook light" or "ghost light" was also used in the United States to describe a slightly different phenomenon – the "weird American cousin" of the European jack-o'-lantern, if you will. In many areas of the United States, residents witnessed stationary balls of light that would wax and wane depending on time and season. These were most often caused by leaks from naturally occurring methane or phosphine gas deposits underground, or off-gassing from decaying organic matter in moist, low-lying areas; in certain areas, atmospheric and meteorological conditions also played a role. The same solutions were often given to explain away the classic jack-o'-lantern, but there was one major difference: old-school jack-o'-lanterns moved quickly and erratically, often covering great distances, and it's hard to square such activity with static gas deposits.

African-American Traditions

The traditional European jack-o'-lantern legend was also quickly embraced – and transformed – by African-Americans and integrated into their complex system of superstition and folklore. They were known as "jacky-mi-lanterns" or "wuller-wups" and often portrayed as sinister, monstrous creatures straight out of an H.P. Lovecraft story, though echoes of the original Scotch-Irish legends remain. Writing in *British Goblins* in 1880, Wirt Sikes noted, "The negroes of the southern seaboard states of America invest the goblin with an exaggeration of the horrible peculiarly their own. They call it Jack-muh-lantern, and describe it as a hideous creature five feet in height, with goggle eyes and huge mouth, its body covered with long hair, which goes leaping and bounding the air like a gigantic grasshopper. This frightful apparition is stronger than any man and swifter than any horse, and compels its victims to follow it into the swamp, where it leaves them to die."

Mary A. Owens collected folklore tales from elderly African-American women in Missouri in the late nineteenth cen-

Jack-O'-Lantern

tury. Here are some of their discussions of the jack-o'-lantern, as paraphrased and retold by the folklorist M. J. Walhouse:

> "When men who have been running after other folks' wives have been enticed on amid marshes and drowned, the Devil's old woman goes and catches their spirits, and ties them up in big bladders, and lights them and turns them loose in the bogs and sloughs, and so they fool and entice other sinners into the bogs, making them think they see a man or woman with a lantern; this is the way they draw folks on. There is a man-jacky and a woman-jacky. If a man going along in the night loses the road, he sees in front of him what he is certain is a woman with a lantern. He sees the lantern plain, and he thinks he sees the woman; but he can't see her plain, and he follows and he follows—he can't help it—and he thinks he hears her say something, though he can't tell what, so he follows on through the mud, and down in the slosh he falls, from which he won't get out till the Judgment Day. If a woman lose the road, she imagines she sees a man with a light, and she tries to catch him up, and follows and follows, till down she goes…

> "…The worst kind of jacky- mi-lantuhns don't come out of marshes, but out of grave yards, and stun drowning folk, and then suck out their blood and leave them as dry as husks ; that kind of Wuller-Wups are the worst, because they grow from sucking the life out of creatures till they are as tall as big cotton-wood trees, and the creatures they have sucked to death get up and go on in the same business, and they too grow

and grow, appearing in fiery shape, but all their life is on the outside, and their hearts are as cold as death."[125]

Harry Middleton Hyatt, who interviewed hundreds of African-Americans (many of them former slaves) in the early twentieth century about hoodoo and folklore, was once told by an elderly woman that jack-o'-lanterns were in fact little people, "misshapen and browned-skinned who carried small lanterns with them at night while out hunting. The following day they spent the time cooking what had been caught the preceding evening. They never appeared during the day, and at night if you met them they were harmless." Another informant told him that if your children are out playing at night, you should put an iron poker from the hearth in the fire, which will ensure that the jack-o'-lanterns won't snatch them away.

Chapter 7

The Jack-O'-Lantern in the Twentieth Century

By the dawn of the twentieth century, the pumpkin jack-o'-lantern was a firmly established part of American Halloween celebrations – in fact, it was the star of the show, as central to the holiday as the evergreen tree is to Christmas today. Canned pumpkin (actually winter squash) became a convenient alternative to create pumpkin pies, and more people began to use pumpkins for decorations rather than as a food source. New strains began to be developed with the jack-o'-lantern in mind – they were more ornamental and attractive in nature and easier to carve. The most popular type was (and is) the Howden strain, ubiquitous today as the standard ribbed orange pumpkin, round and symmetrical.

In the pages that follow, I've attempted to put together a rudimentary history of the jack-o'-lantern in twentieth-century America, primarily through vintage photographs I've collected over the years. These pictures document our ongoing and always-changing relationship to this strange folkloric symbol, and how it inspires both fascination and creativity.

David Acord

CHILDREN

As noted earlier, children and jack-o'-lanterns have been inextricably tied together since the 19th century. Carving lanterns was seen as a juvenile activity, as were tricks that involved using the lanterns

Jack-O'-Lantern

to frighten unsuspecting travelers and neighbors. Babies were (and are) also frequently photographed with jack-o'-lanterns, turning the freshly ripe pumpkins into symbols of abundance, new life, juvenile joy and carefree play. These characterizations also harken back to the qualities of the jack-'o'-lantern's earlier faery incarnations, like the will-o'-the-wisp.

David Acord

BEAUTIES

Like the connection with children, another hallmark of the American jack-o'-lantern tradition is the pairing of the carved pumpkin with young, beautiful women. It has been a staple of news photographers and pin-up artists for decades. But why? Again, the connection seems almost primal. Obviously, harvest season (with which modern Halloween coincides) is a time of bounty and abundance, at least in theory. Crops are coming in, fruits are ripening, and the land takes on a new array of color and beauty. The pumpkin symbolizes all of those things; the radiant young woman is the perfect counterpart, embodying youthful exuberance, fertility and promise for the future.

Barbara Hale and friend, Las Vegas, 1956.

Jack-O'-Lantern

Anne Holmes, Maine Harvest Queen, 1935.

David Acord

Girl with jack-o'-lantern in midwest pumpkin patch, 1953.

Jack-O'-Lantern

Jack-o'-lanterns and cheesecake: a winning recipe for decades. Various model publicity photos, c. 1950s.

David Acord

POSTCARDS

Halloween-themed postcards were enormously popular in the first decades of the twentieth century. As it became more "respectable," Halloween was seen as a way for adults, and not just children, to socialize and have fun. The postcards -- thousands of different designs in total -- were a cheap, convenient way for friends and family to stay in touch and acknowledge a new American celebration.

Postcards helped to shape the public perception of Halloween in general and the jack-o'-lantern in particular. Many cards illustrated centuries-old folklore and superstitions for a new generation, while others simply made up new "traditions" and beliefs about the jack-o'-lantern. Many of these latter cards were aimed at young women and emphasized a connection between Halloween and romance.

On the following pages are several examples of the wide variety of jack-o'-lantern-themed postcards, circa 1900-1930s.

Jack-O'-Lantern

Jack-O'-Lantern

Jack-O'-Lantern

HALLOWE'EN PUMPKINS
DESIGN COPYRIGHTED, JOHN WINSCH, 1913.

With pumpkin heads all peering,
Is it not a fearsome sight?
For the witching hour is nearing
Of Hallowe'en midnight!

David Acord

Jack-O'-Lantern

David Acord

YANKEE INGENUITY

As the jack-o'-lantern grew in popularity in the United States, creative types and inventors began conjuring up alternatives to the traditional carved pumpkin with triangle eyes, nose and jagged-toothed mouth.

In the late 1930s, a landscape gardener and nurseryman from Madison, Ohio named John Czeszcziczki ("Mr. CZ" for short) began experimenting with a way to drastically alter the appearance of pumpkins while they grew, without the use of a knife or any other tool. He created two-piece molds made of brass and aluminum that he clamped onto young pumpkins that were still growing. The molds were designed to look like faces of famous celebrities (Great Garbo, Clark Gable) and traditional halloween ghosts and ghouls. As the pumpkins grew, they pushed into the molds and reformed into the likeness. After a couple of weeks, CZ removed the molds and -- voila -- a strange new breed of human-faced pumpkins were born. He sold the pumpkins at local farmers' markets and later patented the process.

Jack-O'-Lantern

John Czeszcziczki with some of his pumpkin creations, Oct. 1938.

DOMESTIC BLISS

By the late 1930s, the mainstreaming of the jack-o'-lantern into modern culture was complete. It was now an indelible piece of Americana, representative of domestic happiness and comfort.

Below: Photo promoting National Flower Week, Oct. 1945.

Facing page, top: 1937 Halloween party place setting.

Facing page, bottom: 1942 Halloween party, complete with World War II military serviceman, home on leave.

Jack-O'-Lantern

David Acord

AMERICANA

Below: High-schoolers paint jack-o'-lanterns on a storefront window, Maple Heights, Cleveland, 1960.

Facing page, top: Every Halloween since 1952, Union Oil (now Phillips 66) has painted its 80,000-barrel storage tank in Wilmington, Calif. to resemble a jack-o'-lantern. It is known as "Smilin' Jack."

Facing page, bottom: In 1944, after the U.S. liberated the Philippines from Japanese occupation, officials organized an "all-American Halloween party" at a local high school to celebrate. Filipino teens carved jack-o'-lanterns out of papayas. The jack-o'-lantern's transformation into an American symbol was complete.

Jack-O'-Lantern

David Acord

THE CHANGING FACE OF THE AMERICAN JACK-O'-LANTERN

Chicago produce salesman Daniel Goodman created a variety of detailed jack-o'-lanterns using other vegetables, like zucchini, for exaggerated facial features (1950).

Jack-O'-Lantern

Child with decorated jack-o'-lanterns at a market, 1960.

In 1956, a manufacturer created a line of ceramic, American-style jack-o'-lanterns to sell in Italy during the All Saints Day celebration on November 1. Unfortunately, the idea didn't really catch on.

David Acord

Jack-o'-lanterns, 1970s-style.

Jack-O'-Lantern

THE PUMPKIN MAN

Throughout the 1950s, Chicago-area florist George Mangel dressed up as "Pumpkin Man" at his large nursey where he sold thousands of pumpkins. Parents brought their children to have their pictures taken, but some were less than enthusiastic about the experience -- and it's not hard to wonder why.

David Acord

Jack-O'-Lantern

PUMPKINVILLE, USA

This Texas pumpkin stand was one of many roadside attractions that sprang up during Halloween season. The pictures below are from the late 1930s.

David Acord

POLITICAL JACK-O'-LANTERNS

Over the years, jack-o'-lanterns have been used to express a vairety of political views as well as creative impulses. Below, a pair of pumpkins representing Hitler and Stalin, created on the brink of world war in 1939.

Jack-O'-Lantern

In 1971 the White House staff had a pumpkin-carving contest and created likenesses of President Richard Nixon (top left), Spiro Agnew (bottom right) and other political figures of the day.

CONCLUSION: THE JACK-O'-LANTERN IN THE 21st CENTURY

In 1834, Jabez Allies wandered into the English countryside in search of ancient dinosaur tracks. Instead, he found a wealth of stories about strange lights enticing travelers off the main roads after dark. The locals called these lights jack-o'-lanterns, among many other names. What Allies didn't know – couldn't know – was that within a few decades, those lights would be all but extinct in Great Britain, thanks to changes in agricultural methods and the widespread drainage of low-lying farmland. The superstitions associated with them – both pagan and Christian – would fade from popular memory soon after, as well.

But the name itself refused to die. The jack-o'-lantern as a concept, an identity, moved on to new forms – first carved turnips, then carved pumpkins. New generations created new stories and superstitions about it. What was once feared became an endearing symbol of childhood, nostalgia, and dim memories of ancient beliefs.

The jack-o'-lantern was always on the move, as well. It packed up and came to America with the first waves of Scoth-Irish immigrants and, once here, allowed itself to be reshaped and reformed by new citizens of a new country. It was adopted as a Halloween mascot and, by the middle of the 20th century, was a ubiquitous presence each October – from actual carved pumpkins to plastic replicas used to hold children's trick-or-treat candy. No one was afraid of it anymore.

In the 21st century, the jack-o'-lantern is on the move once again, morphing before our very eyes. Festivals devoted it are held each October across the country. The simple act of carving a pumpkin has turned into a bonafide art form; each year talented craftsmen and women find new ways to express their creativ-

Jack-O'-Lantern

Photo credit: Stefan Munder

ity through ever-more-complex jack-o'-lantern creations (see pictures on these and following pages). Its pagan and religious trappings gone, the jack-o'-lantern is now a muse to artists everywhere, literally a shining example of what one can do with a little talent, a lot of hard work and a humble garden-variety fruit.

Where the jack-o'-lantern goes next is impossible to tell. Will it one day reclaim its spookier and more sinister reputation from centuries past? Or will it continue to serve as a bright, happy symbol of a holiday that becomes more popular (and less removed from its ancient past) every year? Stay tuned. Meanwhile, enjoy the show.

David Acord

Jack-O'-Lantern

Photo credits:
bernard_in_va,
Holtorf Pumpkin
Carving Association,
Vienna, VA.

Endnotes

1   Allies, Jabez. *Observations on Certain Curious Indentations in the Old Red Sandstone of Worcestershire and Herefordshire*, pp. 55-64. London: William Edwards, c. 1835.

2   Ibid.

3   Ibid.

4   Allies, Jabez. *On the Ignis Fatuus, or Will-O'-the-Wisp, and the Fairies*, pp. 1-3. London: Simpkin, Marshall and Co., 1846.

5   Brand, John. *Observations on the Popular Antiquities of Great Britain, Vol. III*, p. 397. London: George Bell and Sons, 1901.

6   Scott, Charles P.G. "The Devil and his Imps: An Etymological Inquisition" in *Transactions of the American Philological Association, Volume XXVI*, pp. 79-146. Boston: Ginn & Company, 1895.

7   Stapylton, Robert. *The Slighted Maid*, Page 49. 1663. Text online: http://quod.lib.umich.edu/e/eebo/A61309.0001.001?rgn=main;view=fulltext

8   *The Times* (London, England), Tuesday, July 15, 1828, p. 2.

9   Allies, Jabez. *On the Ignis Fatuus, or Will-o-the-Wisp, and the Fairies*, p. 15. London: Simpkin, Marshall and Co., 1846.

10   Skeat, Walter William. *An Etymological Dictionary of the*

English Language, p. 353. Oxford: Clarendon Press, 1898.

11   *The Evening Post* (New York, New York), Friday, March 9, 1838, p. 3.

12   "Peace Meeting at Heywood." *Empire* (Middlesex, London), Monday, April 9, 1855, p. 310.

13   *The Freeman's Journal or The North-American Intelligencer* (Philadelphia, Pennsylvania), Wednesday, Feb 15, 1792, p. 2.

14   *Democratic Pharos* (Logansport, Iowa, Wednesday, August 14, 1844, p. 1.

15   *The Rockingham Register* (Harrisonburg, Virginia), July 15, 1892.

16   Scott, pp. 116-117, 125.

17   Scott, p. 90.

18   This list of alternate names for the jack-o'-lantern was compiled from numerous sources, including *British Goblins* by Wirt Sikes (Sampson Low, 1880, p. 19); Brand, pp. 395-411; Scott, pp. 79-146; Allies' *On the Ignis Fatuus*, pp. 3-18; *Brownies and Bogles* by Louise Imogen Guiney (Boston: D. Lothrop, 1888, pp. 109-122); "Collection of English Proverbs of the Twelfth Century," in *Cochrane's Foreign Quarterly Review*, No. II, March 1835, p. 383; *The Reader's Handbook of Allusions, References, Plots and Stories* by E. Cobham Brewer (London: Chatto & Windus, 1890, pp. 485-486); and "The Will-O'-the-Wisp and Its Folklore," in *The Gentleman's Magazine*, Jan.-June 1881, pp. 336-342.

19 "The Folk-Lore of Shakespeare," William Thoms. *The Daguerrotype*, 1847 – Vol. 1, p. 364.

20 Brewer, p. 486 (see at 18).

21 "Ignis Fatuus," Fernando Sanford. *The Scientific Monthly*, Volume 9, October 1, 1919, pp. 359-360.

22 Mavor, William Fordyce. *A General Collection of Voyages and Travels...*, Vol. 15, p. 223. London: Sherwood, Neely, and Jones, 1813.

23 "Will-O'-The-Wisp." *The Penny Magazine of the Society for the Diffusion of Useful Knowledge*, 1845, Volume 14, pp. 266-67.

24 Houston, Edwin James. *The Wonder Book of the Atmosphere*, pp. 274-280. New York: Frederick A. Stokes, 1907.

25 *The Times* (London, Greater London, England), Friday, Feb. 22, 1828, Page 3.

26 "Will-O'-The-Wisp." *The Penny Magazine of the Society for the Diffusion of Useful Knowledge*, 1845, Volume 14, p. 266.

27 Sikes, Wirt. *British Goblins,* pp. 18-19. Boston: James R. Osgood & Co., 1881.

28 Allies, Jabez. *On the Ignis Fatuus, or Will-o-the-Wisp, and the Fairies*, pp. 15-18. London: Simpkin, Marshall and Co., 1846.

29 "Ghost Lights of the West Highlands," R.C. Maclagan, *Folklore*, Vol. 8, 1897, p.221.

Jack-O'-Lantern

30 "Will-O'-The-Wisp," T.L. Phipson. *Belgravia* Vol. VI, October 1868, p. 393.

31 Guiney, p. 124 (see previous footnote) and Scott, p. 126.

32 Allies, Jabez (quoting Hall). *On the Ancient British, Roman and Saxon Antiquities and Folklore of Worcestershire*, p. 426. London: J.H. Parker, 1852.

33 Ibid., p. 427.

34 Croker, Thomas. *Fairy Legends and Traditions of the South of Ireland, Part III*, p. 11. London: John Murray, c. 1827.

35 Allies, Jabez (quoting Hall). *On the Ancient British, Roman and Saxon Antiquities and Folklore of Worcestershire*, p. 427. London: J.H. Parker, 1852.

36 Guiney, p. 123.

37 Croker, pp. 231-232.

38 Scott, p. 127.

39 Scott, p. 128.

40 "Of Brother Rush, and the Wonders He Performed in a Monastery, &c." Wolf, Ferdinand and Stephen Endlicher (ed.). *Foreign Quarterly Review,* October 1836, p. 102.

41 Glanvil, Joseph. *Saducimus Triumphatus: or, Full and Plain Evidence Concerning Witches and Apparitions*, pp. 137, 164. London: J. Collins, 1681.

42   *The Mad Pranks and Merry Jests of Robin Goodfellow*, p. xviii. London: C. Percy (reprint of 1628 edition), undated.

43   "Of Brother Rush, and the Wonders He Performed in a Monastery, &c." Wolf, Ferdinand and Stephen Endlicher (ed.). *Foreign Quarterly Review,* October 1836, p. 106.

44   Keightley, Thomas. *The Fairy Mythology, Illustrative of the Romance and Superstition of Various Countries*, p. 287. London: George Bell & Sons, 1884.

45   *The Mad Pranks and Merry Jests of Robin Goodfellow*, pp. 19-20. London: C. Percy (reprint of 1628 edition), undated.

46   Scott, p. 129.

47   Ibid., p. 21.

48   Ibid., p. 22.

49   Crell, A.F. and Wallace, W.M. *The Family Oracle of Health: Economy, Medicine, and Good Living*, p. 24. London: J. Walker, 1824.

50   "East Anglian Superstitions (conclusion), The Lady Cranworth. *The Eastern Counties Magazine*, Vol. I, No. III (c. 1900-1901), pp. 171-172.

51   Hoare, Christabel. *The History of an East Anglian Soke: Studies in Original Documents*, p. 418. Bedford (England): Beds. Times Publishing Co. Ltd., 1918.

52   Dutt, William A. *Wild Life in East Anglia*, p. 201. London: Methuen & Co., 1906.

53   Allies, Jabez. *Observations on Certain Curious Indentations in the Old Red Sandstone of Worcestershire and Herefordshire*, pp. 55-56. London: William Edwards, c. 1835.

54   Allies, Jabez. *On the Ignis Fatuus, or Will-O'-the-Wisp, and the Fairies*, p. 4. London: Simpkin, Marshall and Co., 1846.

55   Engel, Carl. *Musical Myths and Facts*, p. 207. London: Novello, Ewer & Co., 1876.

56   "The Folk-Lore of Shakespeare," William Thoms. *The Daguerrotype*, 1847 – Vol. 1, p. 364.

57   Thorpe, Benjamin. *Northern Mythology, Comprising the Principal Popular Traditions and Superstitions of Scandinavia, North Germany, and the Netherlands, Vol. III*, p. 220. London: Edward Lumley, 1851.

58   Ibid., p. 86.

59   Thorpe, p. 85.

60   "The Will-O'-the-Wisp and Its Folklore," in *The Gentleman's Magazine*, Jan.-June 1881, p. 344.

61   Ibid., p. 345.

62   Ibid., p. 344.

63   Thoms, p. 364.

David Acord

64   The Will-O'-the-Wisp and Its Folklore," in *The Gentleman's Magazine*, Jan.-June 1881, p. 345.

65   Thoms, p. 365.

66   "The Will-O'-the-Wisp and Its Folklore," in *The Gentleman's Magazine*, Jan.-June 1881, p. 342.

67   Ibid.

68   *Norfolk Archaeology*, pp. 299-301. Old Haymarket (Liverpool): Charles Muskett, 1849.

69   Engel, pp. 207-208.

70   Ibid., p. 343.

71   Ibid., p. 345.

72   Brand, p. 399.

73   "Ghostly Lights," H.F. Feilberg. *Folklore Volume VI*, 1895, pp. 288-290.

74   "Will-O'-The-Wisp," T.L. Phipson. *Belgravia* Vol. VI, October 1868, pp. 397-98.

75   Jones, Edmund. *A Relation of Apparitions of Spirits, In the County of Monmouth, and the Principality of Wales*, pp. v-vi. Newport (Monmouthshire, England): E. Lewis, 1813.

76   "Ghostly Lights," by M.J. Walhouse, *Folklore Vol. V – 1894*, p. 293.

77 Croker, p 79.

78 "An Eerie Superstition," Rev. John Price. *Wales*, Vol II No. 12, April 1895, p. 146.

79 Baring-Gould, Sabine. *A Book of South Wales*, pp. 250-251. London: Methuen & Co., 1905.

80 Ibid, p. 250.

81 "Ghostly Lights," by M.J. Walhouse, *Folklore Vol. V – 1894*, p. 293-94.

82 Jones, p. 78.

83 Ibid., p. 79.

84 Ibid., p. 82.

85 Baxter, Richard. *The Certainty of the World of Spirits Fully Evinced* (1691), pp. 45-46. London: Joseph Smith, 1834 (reprint).

86 "The Ignis Fatuus, Its Character and Legendary Origin," William Wells Newell. *The Journal of American Folklore*, Volume 17, 1904, p. 43.

87 Ibid., p. 46.

88 Crowe, Catherine. *The Night-side of Nature* (1848), pp. 329-330. Philadelphia: Henry T. Coates & Co, 1901 (reprint, new edition w/introduction).

89 "Ghost Lights of the West Highlands," R.C. Maclagan, *Folklore*, Vol. 8, 1897, p.207.

90 Ibid., p. 210.

91 Ibid., p. 204.

92 "Evolution of Light from the Human Body." *Ainsworth Magazine*, Vol. 13, 1848, p. 284

93 Ibid., p. 285.

94 Ibid,., p. 286.

95 Ibid., p. 288.

96 Ibid., p. 289.

97 Ibid., p. 290.

98 "Dead Man's Hand – London Standard." *Current Literature Vol. II – January-June, 1889*, p. 333.

99 Henderson, William. *Notes on the Folk-Lore of the Northern Counties of England and the Borders*, pp. 241-242. London: W. Satchell, Peyton & Co., 1879.

100 Ibid., p. 239.

101 "The Hand and the Master-Finger," Prof. James Mackintosh. *Ballou's Monthly Magazine, Volume 50, July-December 1879*, p.458.

102 Gutch (Mrs.) and Mabel Peacock. *County Folk-lore, Vol. V, Printed Extracts No. VII, Examples of Printed Folk-Lore Concerning Lincolnshire*, p. 109. London: David Nutt, 1908.

103 Mackintosh, p. 454.

104 Feilberg, p. 297.

105 Most of the material in the "Sea Lights" section (except where otherwise cited) was gleaned from Fletcher Bassett's indispensable *Legends and Superstitions of the Sea and of Sailors*, pp. 302-320, Chicago/New York: Belford, Clarke & Co., 1885.

106 "The Ignis Fatuus." *Miners' and Farmers' Journal* (Charlotte, North Carolina), Monday, November 15, 1830, p. 4.

107 Bassett, pp. 302-320.

108 "St. Elmo's Fire." *The New Standard Encyclopedia, Volume Nine*. New York: The University Society, 1907.

109 Bassctt, pp. 302-320.

110 Peacock, Edward. *A Glossary of Words Used in the Wapentakes of Manley and Corringham (Linconshire)*, Volume II, p. 572. London: Trubner & Co., 1889.

111 Allies, Jabez. *On the Ancient British, Roman and Saxon Antiquities and Folklore of Worcestershire*, p. 423. London: J.H. Parker, 1852.

112 Darlington, Thomas. *The Folk Speech of South Cheshire*, p. 412. London: Trubner and Co., 1887.

113 "Hallow E'en," J.K. *The Dew-Drop: A Monthly Magazine for the Young*, Second Series, Volume XI, pps. 5-6. Glasgow: Bruce and Martin, 1873.

114 "AllHallowtide," by M.E. Leicester Addis, in *Frank Leslie's Popular Monthly*, Vol. XL, p. 540.

115 "Down on the Farm – Fellowship Club Meets at Harvest Home Dinner." *The Daily Inter-Ocean* (Chicago), October 19, 1894 (morning edition), p. 1.

116 "Halloween Customs in the Celtic World" (lecture). Prof. Bettina Arnold, October 31, 2001.

117 Frazer, Sir James George. *The Golden Bough: A Study in Magic and Religion*, Volume 6, p. 74. London: Macmillan and Company, 1922.

118 Ott, Cindy. *Pumpkin: The Curious History of an American Icon*, p. 10. Seattle and London: University of Washington Press, 2012.

119 "Out for a Walk," (poem) L.F. Armitage, in Our Little Tot's Speaker, p. 10. Chicago: Imperial Publishing Company, 1899.

120 "Thanksgiving Signs." *The Catholic Advance*, Dec. 2, 1905, Page 2.

121 "Jack-O'-Lantern." *Chicago Tribune*, Nov. 22, 1914, p. 36.

122 "Guy Fawkes Day" in *Encyclopaedia of Superstitions, Folklore, and the Occult Sciences*, Volume 3, p. 1529. Milwaukee: J.H. Yewdale & Sons, 1903.

123 "The Pumpkin Effigy." *Harper's Weekly,* Saturday, November 23, 1867, Page 1.

124 "Foolish Fire," by John Hicks, reprinted in *Skylook*, December 1969, Page 13.

125 "Ghostly Lights" by M.J. Walhouse, in *Folklore*, Vol. V, 1894, pps. 297-98. London: David Nutt.

About the Author

David Acord is a writer, communications professional and former journalist and editor in Washington, DC. He is also the author of *What Would Lincoln Do?* (Sourcebooks, 2008), *Success Secrets of Sherlock Holmes* (Penguin, 2011), *When Mars Attacked: Orson Welles and the Radio Broadcast That Changed America Forever* (2013) and *Graveyard Groove: The Haunted History of Monster Music* (2018).

Contact David at dacord8@gmail.com and follow him on Twitter @CaptainOctober.

Printed in Dunstable, United Kingdom